A TIME IN ROME

Elizabeth Bowen was born in Dublin in 1899, the only child of an Irish lawyer and landowner. She was educated at Downe House School in Kent. Her book *Bowen's Court* (1942) is the history of her family and their house in County Cork, and *Seven Winters* (1943) contains reminiscences of her Dublin childhood. In 1923 she married Alan Cameron, who held an appointment with the BBC and who died in 1952. She travelled a good deal, dividing most of her time between London and Bowen's Court, which she inherited.

Elizabeth Bowen is considered by many to be one of the most distinguished novelists of the twentieth century. Her first book, a collection of short stories, *Encounters*, appeared in 1923, followed by another, *Ann Lee's*, in 1926. *The Hotel* (1927) was her first novel, and was followed by *The Last September* (1929), *Joining Charles* (1929), another book of short stories, *Friends and Relations* (1931), *To the North* (1932), *The Cat Jumps* (short stories, 1934), *The House in Paris* (1935), *The Death of the Heart* (1938), *Look at All Those Roses* (short stories, 1941), *The Demon Lover* (short stories, 1945), *The Heat of the Day* (1949), *Collected Impressions* (essays, 1950), *The Shelbourne* (1951), *A World of Love* (1955), *A Time in Rome* (1960), *After-thought* (essays, 1962), *The Little Girls* (1964), *A Day in the Dark* (1965) and her last book, *Eva Trout* (1969).

She was awarded the CBE in 1948, and received the honorary degree of Doctor of Letters from Trinity College, Dublin, in 1949 and from Oxford University in 1956. In the same year she was appointed Lacy Martin Donnelly Fellow at Bryn Mawr College in the United States. In 1965 she was made a Companion of Literature by the Royal Society of Literature. Elizabeth Bowen died in 1973.

ALSO BY ELIZABETH BOWEN

Encounters
Ann Lee's
The Hotel
The Last September
Joining Charles
Friends and Relations
To the North
The Cat Jumps
The House in Paris
The Death of the Heart
Look at All Those Roses
Bowen's Court
Seven Winters
The Demon Lover
The Heat of the Day
Collected Impressions
The Shelbourne
A World of Love
After-thought
The Little Girls
A Day in the Dark
Eva Trout

Elizabeth Bowen

A TIME IN ROME

V

VINTAGE

Published by Vintage 2003

2 4 6 8 10 9 7 5 3 1

First published in Great Britain in 1959 by
Jonathan Cape

Vintage
Random House, 20 Vauxhall Bridge Road,
London SW1V 2SA

Random House Australia (Pty) Limited
20 Alfred Street, Milsons Point, Sydney
New South Wales 2061, Australia

Random House New Zealand Limited
18 Poland Road, Glenfield,
Auckland 10, New Zealand

Random House (Pty) Limited
Endulini, 5A Jubilee Road, Parktown 2193,
South Africa

The Random House Group Limited Reg. No. 954009

A CIP catalogue record for this book
is available from the British Library

ISBN 0 099 28495 2

Papers used by Random House are natural, recyclable
products made from wood grown in sustainable forests. The
manufacturing processes conform to the environmental
regulations of the country of origin

Printed and bound in Great Britain by
Cox & Wyman Limited, Reading, Berkshire

TO

MY FRIENDS IN ROME

AND TO

KIRK AND CONSTANCE ASKEW

UNDER WHOSE ROOF

IN NEW YORK

THIS BOOK WAS FINISHED

CONTENTS

A TIME IN Rome

I

THE CONFUSION

TOO MUCH TIME in too little space, I thought, sitting on the edge of my bed at the end of the train journey from Paris. Never have I heard Rome so quiet before or since—I had asked for a quiet room, this was it. It was on the fourth floor, at the back. The bed was low, the window was set high up, one half of it framing neutral sky, the other a shabby projection of the building. Colour seemed, like sound, to be drained away. The hour was half past four, the day Tuesday, the month February. I knew myself to be not far from the Spanish Steps, which had flashed past the taxi like a postcard. These anti-

3

climactic first minutes became eternal. My bedroom's old-fashioned double door, with key in the lock and the tab dangling, had been shut behind him by the outgoing porter; stacked on trestles at the foot of the bed here was my luggage for three months. Through a smaller doorway showed the tiles of a bathroom wanly reflecting electric light. I was alone with my tired senses.

The hotel, from what I had seen of it, was estimable and dignified, nothing gimcrack. The corridor, dark and extremely long, had been lined with noble old-fashioned furniture, and in here was more of it, on top of me. Close to my pillows was the telephone, sharing the marble top of a commode with a lamp with the Campidoglio on its shade. After my one thought I felt unequal to any others and lay down flat. The bed-head was in a corner, so I switched on the lamp and tipped up the shade, to continue my reading of a detective story—interrupted just at the crucial point by my train's arrival at Rome station.

When I emerged from the story, darkness had fallen and I was hungry. Taking with me the *Walks in Rome* of Augustus Hare, I left the hotel to look for dinner. In these surrounding little streets, lit up like aquariums and tonight anonymous, saunterers passed me in vague shoals. Restaurant after restaurant was empty; blue-white electricity, hatless hatstands, walls as chalky and void as the tables' napery.

4

Here and there a waiter posed like a waxwork. Spying through glass doors or over blinds, I began to fear something had gone wrong—actually all that had happened was, I was ahead of the Roman dinner-hour. So I ended in yellow-brocaded Ranieri's, where they showed a polished lack of surprise, among foreigners other than myself. Great gilt candelabra were on the chimney-piece, and for each of us a little vase of anemones. But here I was afflicted by something else: it seemed uncouth to read while dinner was served. Stealing a glance now and then at Augustus Hare, I never succeeded in getting further than Dr. Arnold's 1840 letter to his wife: *"Again this date of Rome; the most solemn and interesting that my hand can write, and even now more interesting than when I saw it last."* This was not my first visit to Rome, either.

Next day, I changed my room for an outside corner one, a floor higher. This, with the freshness following on what seemed more absolute than a mere night's sleep, altered the feeling of everything like magic. I found myself up in a universe, my own, of sun-coloured tiled floor, sunny starchy curtains. Noise, like the morning, rushed in at the open windows, to be contained by the room in its gay tranquillity. Roses, bleached by seasons of light, rambled over the cretonne coverings of the two beds. The idea of Rome, yesterday so like lead, this noonday lay on me lighter than a feather. Life at this level had a society of its own: windows across the way, their shutters clamped back, looked pensively, speakingly in at mine.

The quarter in which the Hotel Inghilterra stands is early nineteenth-century. It fills the slight declivity, shallow as the hollow of a hand, between the Pincio and the Corso, and is bisected by the *de luxe* Via Condotti, apart from which the quarter is unassuming. It has acoustics of its own, echoes and refractions of steps and voices, now and then of the throb of a car in low gear nosing its way among the pedestrians. Every narrow street in this network is one-way; the system is dementing to motorists, who do not embroil themselves in it willingly. Radio jazz, a fervent young singer at her exercises, a sewing-machine tearing along, and the frenetic song of a small-caged bird, hooked to a sill, were my sound-neighbours. From top-but-one-storey windows I beheld one crinkled continuous tawny roofline: all the buildings fitted into this quarter, like segments of a finally solved jigsaw, are one as to height as they are in age. They are ochre, which gave off a kind of August glow on to the mild spring-winter morning: on throughout the chilliest time of year smoulders the afterglow of Rome's summers. And my streets, on a grid plan, sunken deep between buildings, also are all alike: sunless, down there, for the greater part of the day, they stretch so far that they fade away at the ends. Small shops, workshops, bars, and restaurants line them, with apartments or offices above. Banal, affable, ripe to become familiar, this was the ideal Rome to be installed in: everything seemed to brim with associations, if not (so far) any of my own. I began to attach myself by so much as looking. Here I was, centred. I dared to hope that all else might prove as simple. It did not.

One trouble is that Rome's north-south axis, the Corso Romano, does not run due north, due south. It slants, thereby throwing one's sense of direction, insofar as one has one, out of the true. The Piazza di Venezia, at one end, is east of the Piazza del Popolo at the other. Then, there are the exaggerated S-curvings of the Tiber: at one minute the river is at one's elbow, the next lost. A stroll along the embankment is one of the least enjoyable in Rome; the dustiest, baldest, most unrewarding. (To stand on a bridge is another thing.) The Tiber is not intended to be followed; only trams do so, and those in very great numbers. They grind by unceasingly, and one does well to take one.

Then again, there are far more than seven hills: how is one to be clear which *the* Seven are? This seems to be one of the primal facts which guidebooks are obstinate in withholding. Viewed from above, from the Janiculum lighthouse or a terrace of the Pincian gardens, Rome as a whole appears absolutely flat, or if anything sunken in the middle, like a golden-brown pudding or cake which has failed to rise. Down again in the city, you register gradients in aching foot-muscles—this does establish that Rome is hilly. Knowledge of Rome must be physical, sweated into the system, worked up into the brain through the thinning shoe-leather. Substantiality comes through touch and smell, and taste, the tastes of different dusts. When it comes to knowing, the senses are more honest than the intelligence. Nothing is more real than the first wall you lean up against sobbing with exhaustion. Rome no more than beheld (that is, taken in through the eyes only) could still be a masterpiece in cardboard—the eye I suppose being of all the organs the most easily infatuated and then jaded and so tricked. Seeing is pleasure, but not knowledge.

In shape the Capitoline and the Palatine are hills unmistakably; so is the Aventine, at the other side of the trough of the Circo Massimo. But the Caelian, Esquiline, Viminal, and Quirinal are ambiguously webbed together by ridges. On the whole I have come to suppose that these *are* the Seven— but if so, what of the Pincian, "hill of garden," and Janiculum, bastion across the river? I asked a number of friends, but no two gave me the same answer; some did not care to be pinned down, others put forward their own candidates. That I should be set on compiling a definitive list of the Seven Hills, eager to check on all, to locate each, was, I can see, disillusioning to people who had hoped I might show

more advanced tastes. So, given the equal unwilling-
ness of guide-books to disgorge anything like a list,
I left Rome, when the end of my time came, no more
certain as to the Seven Hills.

Nor was it only as to those that authorities sent me
away hungry. Nothing was harder to come at than
information; practically no book I read was basic
enough. Sifting through other people's many impressions, I found half-grains, the sheerest modicum,
of established fact. What I was looking for was so
elementary, so much (I suppose) a matter of common knowledge, that no one had considered it worth
recording. What I wanted to know had so long been
known that possibly it had been again forgotten.
I had a continuous craving for lists and dates. Almost everything seemed to have been hazed over. I
could have fancied, as children tend to do, that
here was some adult conspiracy of silence. But of
course my unbearable handicap was my own ignorance. Keats called his ignorance "giant"; mine was
monstrous. To a point perhaps it was occupational:
for a novelist it becomes easier, second nature, to
imagine rather than to learn. Thousands of us would
rather invent than study. As against that it may be
said for writers that they mistrust vagueness, abhor
inaccuracy. So, there could be nothing for me but
finding out, which became exciting because it was
laborious. The little I did find out I am setting down;
and if my discoveries are other people's common-

places I cannot help it—for me they retain a momentous freshness.

What is the shape of the ground underlying Rome? How would it look, I wondered, stripped of the city? By now, what are either ascending cliffs or descending torrents of buildings mask almost everything—true, here is a gorge, there a rock-face or a velvety green hill-profile; but are these "natural" conformations? The heights have been worked on; levelling or terracing, tunnelling and cutting have gone on; the submerged landscape makes itself felt as man-made, calculated—yet again other contours are due to subsidences, collapses, layers of rubble and ruin choking valleys or clothing themselves in soil and becoming slopes. And as against the blunted creases and hollows there are sharp depths opened by excavation. Falls of *régimes,* wishes to obliterate or to reinstate, have caused these bemusing differences of level, this impossibility of pinpointing any *one* time. Mussolini shaved away a mediaeval quarter to expose a forum; the Colosseum squats where was Nero's lake. Whether history in action has added to the understructure of Rome, or by gnawing away at it worn it down, it is hard for an uninstructed person to know. The effect is of something pressed between two forces, ambition and destruction. In all the convulsive hill country ringed around it, nothing seems so volcanic as Rome.

The Past is either an abstraction or a selected

time: when one gives it a capital P it becomes the former. It is in nature (at least in mine) to make for the concrete and particular, to "choose" a time and reconstitute, if one can, one or another of its moments. Happenings are objective; the effect of them never can quite evaporate. In Rome I wondered how to break down the barrier between myself and happenings outside *my* memory. I was looking for splinters of actuality in a shifting mass of experience other than my own. Time is one kind of space; it creates distance. My chafing geographical confusion was in a way a symptom of inner trouble—my mind could not be called a blank, for it tingled with avidity and anxieties: I was feeling the giddiness of unfocused vision. There came no help from reason, so I was passive. It is one way of approaching, to be passive, to be attracted in inexplicable directions, then half-see why. It takes one's entire capacity to live one moment—the present, the moment one *is* living. One is enclosed in that, there can be no other. But cannot the present serve as a reflector?

To talk of "entering" the past is nonsense, but one can be entered by it, to a degree. All happenings, whatever their place in time, must have *as* happenings something in common—whatever went on, goes on, in one form or another. One can more than picture, one can all but take part. History is not a book, arbitrarily divided into chapters, or a drama chopped into separate acts: it has flowed forward. Rome is a continuity, called "eternal." What has accumulated in this place acts on everyone, day and night, like an extra climate.

That was the climate I felt first. I had come here knowing no Roman history; what I must have learned at school had been overlaid. I have no Latin.

Difficulties with the map . . . The one I bought, the Nuovissima Pianta, had been impossible to avoid —pressed upon me at every counter, by every vendor. Very newest it may have been, but not satisfactory. It is large, and I was in a constant state of needing to unfurl it in its entirety. Not canvas-backed, it is printed on brittle paper which disintegrates almost before you touch it. Rome throughout February into March is windy, draughts if there are not gusts, gusts if there are not outright gales: the Pianta forever was rearing up to wrap itself blindingly round my face. My struggles with it were acute in the early days when I needed its guidance at every corner. Breakfast-hour sessions with the Pianta, in the sunny lull of my room with windows shut, failed to carry me through the ensuing day: I am unable to memorize any route. Again and again, while I was out walking, I turned aside into cafés; over some tiny table the Pianta could be draped like a limp cloth—in such pauses I could at least establish where I was not, or how far from where I had hoped to be. Rome seemed an often-shaken kaleidoscope. And a would-be attraction of the Pianta's is its featuring of principal monuments as drawings. Outsize façades blot out, each time, the street-network in their vicinity, so that ways of approach to them or departure from them cannot be traced. One is left to guesswork.

For this reason, I lost my way on leaving the Pantheon, my second afternoon. In a hurry to keep an appointment better not made, I believed myself to be headed for the Corso Romano, when, without warning, the Largo Argentina, excavated temples, trees, theatre, taxi rank and all, burst upon my horrified gaze. Nothing should have been wrong with the Argentina: simply I had had no idea of Rome's containing anything of the sort. I could not have been more badly thrown out of gear if I had found myself really in South America. Nor had I grasped till then that there are *two* Corso's, the other being the Vittore Emanuele.

Simply coming to Rome cannot be half so complex as coming back. This time, I was making anything but a clean start. I was in the hold of memories as positive and obsessive as they were faulty. I was constantly brought up short with, "I could have *sworn* . . . !" Ingrained pictures refused to be broken up; I had lived with them, lived on them, for how many years? Trite as they were, poor as they came to seem (held up, that is, against the reality), they had been "Rome" for me. What I recollected could not be found again: it had not existed. There came points when I wondered, where was my sanity? Memory must be patchy; what is more alarming is its face-savingness. Something in one shrinks from catching it out—unique to oneself, one's own, one's claim to identity, it implicates one's identity in its fibbing. Proust remarks, creative wrong-memory is a source of art. Good: but when it deceives one about a city this trickiness is a plague and the very devil. It succeeded in tying up Rome for me into unnecessary, dismaying knots. Many of my squabbles with the Pianta arose from its contradictions of my subjective map. . . . I never forgave the amiable Largo Argentina, however often I saw it later on. No familiarity caused it to lose its air of being a hallucination in broad daylight.

Actual changes in Rome must be disconcerting— the hacking of new perspectives through old streets, the vanishing of gardens, and so on. Mussolini's theatricalities, few thank him for; what seems less well known is that Garibaldi, in rash old age, sponsored an attempt to straighten the Tiber, which meant carving away an obtruding curve of the gardens of the adorable Villa Farnesina. One man's improvement is another man's poison. Trams, for instance, anguished Augustus Hare, who bewails "mutilation" in their interest. Yet, though grievous, actual changes are less eerie than the fictitious ones. The

Colosseum, I could have sworn, had shifted its position since I last saw it; I wasted a morning in angry search for it. But humiliation, having brought me to tears, gradually eased off into humility. Among Rome's splendours is its unexpectedness, or better, unexpectability. If one cannot enjoy this, one enjoys nothing. Not that I was willing to be got the better of altogether. Partly I crept up on the city, partly attacked it—in the sense of attacking a vast problem. My object was to walk it into my head and (this time) keep it there. To encompass the whole of it was worth trying, as is so much which is impossible. Each day, I reduced some hitherto nebulous area by at least a little. My approach was pedestrian twice over: still, there could be no other. Rome made this so.

Other cities gain by factitious mystery; great portions of them seem to be made of gauze—even for those who inhabit them, work in them, they solidify in regions and patches only. For the visitor they are ideal for this reason. His very hurry electrifies the romance, which will by no means be over when he departs—his dreams are to be haunted for evermore by glimpsed secrets, by-ways left unexplored, arcades unentered, streets he never went down. Architectural mirages, phantasmagoric views from the taxi window ensnare his fancy up to the last moment. Beyond that, London is better left to sink into dusk, Paris to dissolve into misty sunshine. Such

15

capitals gain by subjective treatment, to which they lend themselves.

Rome does not. Rome is anti-romantic; its huge unimaginative, unimaginable forms are by nature daylit, sharp even after dark. Here is an enmity to mystery, a blow, a succession of blows struck at it. Everything stares hard at one; the breakages of the ruins have brutal angles. Is it because of this that Rome is declared by some to have little "atmosphere"? Its positiveness antagonizes one kind of stranger, who goes away feeling overborne; the impressions forcing themselves upon him will have been bossy, discordant, harsh. Often the short-term visitor leaves Rome gladly, nor dare one blame him—opulent as to time, the city is scornful of any lack of it: *that* is the one form of poverty Rome treats badly, with the uncomprehending insolence of the wealthy. In my case, never until now had I had a sum of time to spend.

To the end, I never quite parted company with the Pianta; its uses however began to alter. Every evening, when it and I came back again to the hotel or the Antico Caffè Greco, I engraved that day's route on it in blue pencil, scoring the wretched paper with arrows, circles, *x*'s, and stars. My original copy of the Pianta, having early writhed itself into tatters and broken into sections along the foldings, gave out completely under the pencil-diggings; as in turn, as quickly, did its successors. I had to replace the Pianta five or six times. Each fresh copy carried fresh crops of markings: *had* the thing only been durable, I could have watched my pattern embroider itself as a whole on one. My guide-book, Nagel's, offered maps of a sort, ribbon-thin strips folded in at the end, but it was a fidgety business mating the edges, and vacuums came into being where I did not. Less baffling section-by-section maps, together with plans of buildings and informative diagrams, are contained in the Touring Club Italiano's invaluable *Roma e Dintorni,* a volume fatter than Nagel's for good reason, and well worth any difficulties with Italian. Nobody should be without *Roma e Dintorni* —I was, till near the end of my stay.

Many of my difficulties were unnecessary. If not altogether of my making, they must have arisen out of my character. If they seemed to dog me, this may have been because I had not it in me to avoid them. Early troubles could have been circumvented, but that in itself would have taken trouble—and I dare say the answer was, they did not trouble me. There was a prodigality about those blunders. Mistaken convictions, false starts, plunges in wrong directions —why disown them when I cannot regret them? Without them, Rome would have been less mine. And caught in the meshes of my confusion, like diamonds glittering in a twisted drag-net, were moments I would not for anything have missed.

Hard to form any idea of is the size. From being

so much larger than one expects, Rome seems larger than it probably is. Hills contain it no longer; it overflows, darting all ways like quicksilver. Its onset upon the surrounding country is haphazard, involving a rushing scene-shifting, in the course of which much gets left behind from the act before. In places the effect is that of a cut-out: *modernissimo* apartment-blocks, like photographs, pasted on to a Victorian sepia wash-drawing of small cataracts, olives, and *contadini*. Fragments of balustrade, vestiges of arbours, a farmhouse slatternly and tawny, a shepherd on a hillock among sheep continue to occupy vacant lots or triangles of space between concrete roadways. And the new tones down almost as fast as it has gone up: outdone in bigness and baldness by today's, yesterday's prodigies weather, acclimatize, and begin to take on a veteran air. Rome ingorges whatever is added to it; there seems no end to its power to assimilate—in this whole amalgam, nothing is not Roman: this is true of the buildings caking the one-time marshes, of those stacked up hills or tottering along skylines. The patchwork gains in effect by striking contrasts: Parioli, speckless on its expensive heights, looks besieged by the blotchy tenements down below. This soil must be friendly to builders, as is other to gardeners; few foundations planted have failed to root. Humdrum, dusty, tram-clanging, middle-aged streets and squares seem as firmly embedded as the antique core.

Rome's staid residential districts I did remember, but not their extensiveness or, on me, effect. Latin equivalent of the Victorian, they bespeak a sort of bilious prosperity. The stucco of the stand-offish, secretive houses has darkened from ivory to buff, buff to mustard; their surrounds are metallic ever-green gardens. Sometimes, inside a railing, sounds the costive drip of a fountain not quite turned off. The palm trees look stuffy and un-Southern; any windows not masked by venetian shutters exude gloom through their hangings of clotted lace—not only is it impossible to see in, it must be all but impossible to see out. I eyed the electric bells in their polished circles, wondering who had ever the nerve to press them: few or none are signs of coming-and-going—are the young always out, perhaps, the old always in? One will know nothing about these house-holders till information is graven on to their tomb-stones, which also may carry their photographs glazed on marble. Already there is something cemetery-like about the alignment—though in fact the favoured Campo Verano is very much more viva-cious, alert, and chatty; *there* in some silent way the silence is broken. . . . I do know, almost all Con-tinental cities show these particular rings of social growth; simply in Rome their monstrousness strikes one more. They demand their novelist. Also they are among Rome's everlasting hints of a charnel underside. Already they are being gashed at along their frontiers; knocking down goes on where a site on a through-traffic road has soared in value. For instance, Via Nomentana lets a draught of peril through an entire quarter: there spring up garages, cinemas, chromium bars, catch-penny little shops— so far, no more than a gaudy façade to backwoods of blind windows and caged gardens. Conscious of temerity as I roved and dawdled, trying to peer through lace or contorted ironwork, I felt, as never before in Rome, extraneous, dubious, an alien.

Other days, I sought the opposite extreme, the spearhead vertical suburbs of the Campagna: lean young skyscrapers jumbled on one another like pyramids of cosmetics or tinted candy—white, lemon, orange, apricot, rose, blue-pink, chalk-blue, henna, pistachio, olive, mulberry, violet. Some ape New York, others Scandinavia. Shiny with glass, honeycombed with balconies spawning flowerpots, these appear to be settings for youthful marriages (*rentier*). Many of them sprout out of raw ground, tire-tracked where there are not yet roadways. A representative group may be viewed from the Appian Way, across the foreground of tombs and cypresses; there are also clusterings at the northern outlets. Savagely as they are objected to, they key in with Rome's general virtuosity, and in the distance at sun-

set they look ethereal. . . . The same cannot be
said of the huge glum housing-scheme on the way
out to the "1942" Exhibition—in this each block,
many-floored as a prison and as mean as to windows, has the look of being solid all through. The
ensemble is coloured opaque khaki, and, linked by
archways and having its own shops, is evidently an
effort at unit-planning for families lately into the
middle class. Built at a height, it frowns out over the
country towards the disastrous Exhibition. . . .
Across Rome, where the Via Nomentana in full
spate bridges the Florence-Ancona railway line,
there has been an outburst of what looks like Ger-
manic neo-mediaevalism: the tracks are overhung
for some way along by tall yet somehow whimsical
buildings, topped by gables which seem to expect
storks. . . . Gasworks, slaughter-houses, rubbish
dumps, cattle markets, an abandoned shooting gallery, a defunct racecourse, duststorms of demolition,
skeletal battles of construction, schools, asylums
and hospitals, squatters' villages, marble-works, and
other relics of pleasure or signs of progress crop
up according to where one goes. Each demands to
be taken into the picture. Crazy or neat, no structure is out of use; if it has lapsed from one it has
found another.

This I came to realize: the present-day shape of
Rome has as framework the ancient roads of the

Republic. Their rayings outward account for the starfish growth of the city outside the walls, development having always followed them. Their historic names, on the motorist's route map, now stand for speedways numbered from one to eight. These constitute the directions, and one should master them. They are to be conceived of as darts hurled, from the column in the Forum Romanum, outward to ports on the two seas, the Italian provinces, and, as it came into being, the Empire outside Italy. Their names are Aurelia, Cassia, Flaminia, Salaria, Tiburtina, Prenestina (once Praenestina), Appia, Ostiense (once Ostiensis). And two more have place in the ancient concept: Nomentana, which, headed by its makers for Nomentum in the Sabine Hills, is today a suburban thoroughfare, and Asinaria, long ago faded out—even its destination becomes uncertain. As against that, the today popular Casilina seems to have no notable past.

Aurelia runs north-west to the Mediterranean; originally it served to connect with Rome the then lively coastal towns of Etruria. Following, at varying distances, the seaboard, sometimes swerving inland to circumnavigate mountain gorges, *Aurelia* carries the motorist of today to the Italo-French frontier near Ventimiglia. It was the marching and baggage route to the prospering Roman cities in Provence. Seen the other way round, it provided entrance for travellers who, before railways, took ship to Civitavecchia then proceeded into the capital by coach —at a memorable point, the dome of St. Peter's would jolt into sudden though long-expected view. . . . *Cassia* splits off from *Flaminia* to the north of Rome: *Cassia* goes to Florence via Viterbo. *Flaminia*, by which ones goes to Perugia, was constructed by C. Flaminius, consul, in 223 B.C., to arrive at Ariminum (Rimini) on the Adriatic. *Salaria*, the old salt-carrying route, is the third road northward; it follows the Tiber valley upward for some way, then strikes off into the Sabine country.

Tiburtina is familiar to visitors as the road to Tivoli—once Tibur, where in the Alban hills discriminating Romans had summer villas. *Praenestina* (now Prenestina) took patricians to another resort, Praeneste, where cool air was also to be enjoyed and the splendid temple mounted the hill in terraces. The today Palestrina's excavations are high-and-dry over the glossy motor route—one way to Naples, through Frosinone. Alternative way to Naples, the more crowded, is that which begins as the Via Appia Nuova, goes by the airport then takes eagle upward sweeps into bridge-linked hill towns, the Castelli Romani, after which it goes down again—not till Terracina does this road touch the coast.

With *Appia Antica* (the Appian Way) Appia Nuova has little but name in common; the two leave Rome, even, from different points—though for some miles of their way across the Campagna they run within sight of each other, parallel, in dramatic contrast. . . . With *Ostiensis* (now Ostiense) we are more or less back round the clockface to *Aurelia*. Ostiensis' function was to link Rome with Ostia, when that city-port flourished at the mouth of the Tiber. *That* Ostia today is Ostia Antica: its stretch of river-deserted ruins is by-passed by new Ostiense, "Via del Mare"—which, flanked by its keen competitor the electric railway, is a virtual racing-track to Lido di Roma.

The passion of Romans for getting out of Rome strikes one. I wondered, is it hereditary? Most of the city's present-day population is, I learned, Roman for only a few generations back—if that. But there can be adoptive heredity, I suppose? Becoming Roman, one does as the Romans did; unawares, habits root in antiquity, and the eight great roads seem dedicated all to one purpose: exodus. Reasons for getting out are among the constants of Roman history—danger from personal enemies; an exposed conspiracy; civil disturbance; noxious weather; pestilence; persecution or pogrom; need to tone up in fresh air or reflect in calm; spleen; fashion; annoyance by barbarians; banishment; military or administrative duties; care of country estates; health; imminent scandal; financial crisis. A whole range, back through how many centuries, between desire and compulsion. There were those who set off enjoyably in the cool morning; under cover of night, there were those who slid out—tense, anonymous, cloaked. Slaves fled; their betters "withdrew from Rome." Exits when not dangerous were costly. Also, the destination needed to be property of one's own, or at least a friend's: some remote-enough villa, comfortable hiding. Those who left by choice expected, and could command, a delightful altitude with a view, shade on the scorching hillside, a nearby spring, a shrine, sometimes a temple. The take-off, in state, along fashionable Praenestina or Tiburtina would involve a dashing equipage, with a no less impressive train of lumbering baggage wagons.

Only secondarily were the major roads for family transit or pleasure travel. The eight were not only arteries, they were a nerve-network, connecting the brain, Rome's centre, with the extremities. They were channels for action and means of government. Priorities were military, administrative, commercial. Legions on the move along all the eight, haulage between Rome and the seaports along Aurelia and Ostiensis, salt-porterage along Salaria, emissaries forging north up Cassia and Flaminia, functionaries in progress, messengers posting—all this and more is to be envisaged. And the roads, as they do today, must have streamed with sheep.

Metal-bound wheels on the great stone paving-blocks, hoof-echoes, thunderous trampling, commands, altercations, lashings must have made a road reverberate miles off. Silence could be nowhere in its vicinity. Now, once out of Rome into the open, there *is* near-silence. A plane circling Ciampino, a Vespa throttled, a country cart rattling home cut, sharp, into the soft mechanical hum, so dispersed, so monotonous, so much part of the air that it is more to be felt than heard. Traffic glitters, out across the Campagna, and among the ruin-shadows you stand and watch it—rubberized, it seems to be fanned along.

But the main change now is, everyone can get out. No longer is exodus for the favoured only. At last the general passion has found expression— how long overdue, you see from Sundays and holidays. Family cars overflow, doors strained on their hinges; rakish cut-price taxis are as elastic. Outriders, swarms of bachelors are on Vespas. But the core of the revolution is public transport—I know of no system more far-reaching than Rome's, more energetic or more capacious: hilarious buses, electric road-railways zooming into the hills in ascending spirals, small eager trains darting from stop to stop across reclaimed marshlands or to the coast. One way or another, thousands hurl themselves forth: compared to this, outgoings from other cities seem feeble dribbles. Rome, on Sundays and holidays, empties itself like a tipped-up bucket into Frascati, Tivoli, the Castelli Romani, on to beaches, in anything like summer, or sheltered, made-musical lake shores. On a good day, the sign of a good resort is that it runs out of breathing-space from noon on. Sun cooks the packed-in eaters in glassed-in restaurants. High-hanging municipal terraces mill with admirers of the panorama, elbowing their ways to the parapets for a better view—for, to the interest of spotting Rome in the far distance is added the triumph of being out of it.

Is this passion infectious? It did affect me. To say, no sooner was I in Rome than I wondered how to get out of it would be inexact—more, I realized I should not realize I *was* in Rome until I had been out of it then come back again. Character requires an outside view; also, how can one comprehend what remains on top of one? Rome is full of spaces, but all are Rome. Though my original minutes of claustrophobia never repeated themselves, or threatened to, I set about looking for the gates.

I shrink from the feeling of being foreign—who does not? Mine may be a generation with an extra wish to acclimatize, to identify. Anywhere, at any time, with anyone, one may be seized by the suspicion of being alien—ease is therefore to be found in a place which nominally *is* foreign: this shifts the weight. Rome is the ideal environment for a born stranger; one does not, it is true, belong, but one can imitate—here is much to imitate. The injunction to do when in Rome as the Romans do was superfluous: what else is there to do? I copied the Romans

round me, left, right, and centre—themselves they
were unaware of this; I was not. More and more
was I merged into what went on, while still having
little idea what it was about. Strongly I felt what
was tidal in the life of the city: the ebb made me
restless, the flow contented me. My first Sunday, for
instance, remained a lesson: the pleasure I had expected from having the city to myself never really
dawned, or was all but instantly clouded by misgiv-
ing. Left alone with me, Rome turned away its face.

No born Roman likes to be left with Rome. Last
Mass over, the crowds disperse as though at sound
of a curfew. Those who fail to get out show discom-
fiture—like people on the retreat from a rising
flood, they clamber higher and higher, to the heads
of steps, to topmost terraces and escarpments,
whereon they stand gazing frustratedly at the horizon. Young girls, moody, tap with the high heels of
their pink, yellow, or blue kid shoes, as though their
being nowhere but here reflected in some way upon
their escorts, which it may. Those kept in Rome by
poverty manage better; the working classes give
themselves over to not working—they yawn, take a
look at Sunday, then go to ground. Not more than
one or two outings, for large-sized families, are possible in a year. Many go to bed. Sour sunless courtyards between the tenements fill up like reservoirs
with a lull of nothingness—here or there a cat
crouches or glides, or a tempest of children rushes

from door to door. Now and then through a window comes a groan or a creak. Sunset brings people on to the streets again, with the look in their eyes of depth swimmers surfacing. Few courtyards do not boast a son boasting a Vespa, and as night sets in these come roaring home.

The gates in the wall of Rome, though much extends beyond them, are important. Almost all traffic must pass through one or another. Ancient-Roman in origin, the gates have, most of them, undergone change of name—through several of them saints walked to their martyrdom; one continues to honour its Papal donor; two serve to christen the quarters in which they stand. They are: *Popolo*, formerly Flaminia; *Pinciana; Pia*, formerly Nomentana; *San Lorenzo*, formerly Tiburtina; *Maggiore*, formerly Praenestina; *San Giovanni*, nearby the site of the vanished Porta Asinaria; *Metronia; Latina; San Sebastiano*, formerly Appia; *Ardeatina*, now no more than a name and a gap for traffic; *San Paolo*, formerly Ostiensis. These all are south of the Tiber. Across the Tiber, gates are fewer and play less part: the three to be noted are *Portese, San Pancrazio*, formerly Aurelia, and *Cavelleggeri*.

Strictly, the gates are gateways; they consist of double, triple, or multiple arches. Built or re-architected at different epochs, they vary accordingly in character—the earlier are fortified by towers, the

29

later glorified by façades. Each creates round itself its own kind of neighbourhood. But the dominant is the Aurelian Wall, which the gates no more than punctuate and diversify—once having found the Wall I could not forget it, or be unaware of its continuity. Its re-emergences into view, out of covering buildings, never are not dramatic: whether in view or not it is *there*, and shapes one's sense of the city. Once contained, in essence Rome is so still. There is concentration, only, within the Wall.

This particular psychic concentration is not a matter of architectural bulk—extra-mural Rome is, as a matter of fact, not only larger in acreage than the inner city but more heavily built up. The Wall encloses much that is not urban: grassiness, public and private gardens, tree-shaded domains that could be woods. It is outside, often, that the out-and-out urbanism begins—all the same, with unboundedness goes a sort of dilution: the air seems thinner. Modernity cannot always account for this; the wall by no means is a dividing line between old and new, or older and newer—internal Rome blazes into the twentieth century; external Rome has old-world, lingering patches. No, but for all that the Wall seals in the Rome we recognize as "eternal"—so much so that surfaces, sounds, and smells differ, according to whether one is outside or in. Led blindfold, I swear, I could still tell whether or not I had passed through one of the gates.

The Aurelian Wall is an aid to Roman geography: sights or objects of which one is in search should be related (when one studies the map) to one or another point in its circumference. There is a satisfaction in walking under it—I cannot in words convey its *effect* of height (many things must be higher in reality) or varying flushes of colour, rose-cornelian. Substantiality is in itself a beauty. To brush up against the Wall, or to press one's hand against any part of its surface, is a pleasure. On, on goes the ripple of angles, the buttresses in somnolent repetition—guard towers, stairways, arcaded sentry-walks wait, hollow, idle, endless, to be explored. San Sebastiano gateway and a section adjoining are on view to sight-seers, but I did not ring the custodian's bell—elsewhere one may scale about unofficially, unhindered.

The Wall south of the Tiber describes a loop, outward from the river. Its course, which zigzags hardly less than the river's, begins by the Porta del Popolo, ends just short of the Ponte d'Industria—the thing is like a many-jointed screen, here and there folded into outstanding angles. North of the Tiber, the Wall resumes, *not* opposite where it left off, but three bridges upstream: from the Porta Portese its greek-key pattern mounts to Porta San Pancrazio on the Janiculum. Junction is made with a later, Papal wall, which takes in the Vatican and St. Peter's; fortification on this side ends with the *enceinte* of Castel Sant'

Angelo. Rome across the bridges gives the effect of being more loosely girt than the main city.

To attempt to follow the Wall the whole way round is ambitious—it may be, one loves it the more if one never does. A pleasant stretch of the outer flank, to sample, is from Porta Metronia, along past the Latina and San Sebastiano gates to the Ardeatina traffic-gap: the road is tree-shaded, leisurely, and suburban; there are lawns with benches between the buttresses. Inside, for the corresponding length, are ilexy private gardens, and market gardens—the latter one may enter and wander in, at risk of being chased by a fierce dog. The busy proprietors of the gardens merely gaze, too civil to say one nay: they need not, that is done by their dogs. Here, the arches of the Wall's inner ground-level gallery are in use as potting sheds, stacked with rakes or wired in to contain poultry. A vine trained over an arbour, a lemon tree fruiting beside a cistern among cracked terra-cotta shards remind one that one is, after all, in Italy. Rising from among artichokes and lettuces, particularly in the water-colour light of an early evening, the Wall has the primitive reddish look of a cliff. Many people, however, either do not care to realize that it exists or are unaffected by the fact that it does. Others believe it to be but fragmentary. The Aurelian Wall is played down by guide-books, whose references to it are hurried, oblique, and grudging. This may be because it is one thing too many.

Also, it was a failure. Coming late into Roman history, it was a landmark on the way to decline— a step-down, a symbol of shrinking power. The generation of Romans who watched it rise must have done so with the feeling of degradation with which we behold the drilling of deep shelters: there is a flaw in civilization from the instant it has to admit fear. Rome at its height, that of Augustus, had been an open city—the wall of less certain days had been let lapse, obsolete, unrequired. Barbarians were not an Augustan problem; not till the later half of the third century A.D. was an Emperor, Aurelian, so unfortunate as to find himself faced with them as a menace. He set to work on the Wall, with a realism which made him unpopular. And the irony was, when the crisis finally came, the Wall was not stormed; instead, the cunning barbarian cut the aqueducts. First and last, from the point of view of defence this great construction never succeeded: when not outwitted it was betrayed—hastily re-fortified to resist what in some cases were shattering false alarms, it stood on sturdily into the nineteenth century, only to show itself an anachronism: the French bombarded it, breached it, and swarmed through. Yet this vain strength somehow remains untarnished.

The French failed, at least, to force the Flaminian gate. This stands and long has stood at the head of the wide Via Flaminia, leading to the one ancient bridge still in use: the Pons Milvius, nowadays Ponte Molle. The bridge bore the Via Flaminia over the Tiber, at the start of its resolute northern course. Roman roads are said still to echo the tramp of legions—or so I was told, as a child in Britain. Actually *on* any great road from Rome, who would think of putting ear to the ground? Aurelia, Cassia, Flaminia, Salaria, Tiburtina, Praenestina, Appia, Ostiensis do not run classically straight: forging forward where they have nothing to meet but plains, they are deflected by rocky, defiant hills. But they still feel wire-taut; carried forward by what they carry along, the everlasting incitement of their purpose. Prototype roads, they wheel around in the space which encircles Rome—north into Corot valleys with sky-blue streams; south across the Campagna among sheep, interrupted aqueducts, factories, shadows of clouds; west to the Etruscan Mediterranean; east through the Sabine defiles to the Adriatic. Roads do not sing, but one has a singing sense of them. I walked out of Rome for part of the way on each, only to find myself worsted by the distances: march one might on these roads, but otherwise—no. They are now for motoring. There has opened for them a latent, unforeseen destiny. Outside Rome, do as I did: never refuse a day in a friend's car.

Speed sublimates, melting repetitive advertisements, gargantuan trios of tin red roses, black griffins rampant on yellow banners, into fluid ribbons, also unweaving skylines, liquefying stoniness into lakes, powdering changing heights with more and more unattainable little towns like sun-splashes. So, the force of the roads comes at one in entirety, with a rush.

The Via Appia Antica should not be travelled any way but on foot. (The pity is, paving-stones are being surfaced over.) And inside Rome, I repeat, to be anything but walking is estrangement. Trams, buses, tempting on a return journey, take routes which obliterate one's tracks. Greatest annihilator is a taxi; to collapse into one is to admit defeat—each has a Rome of its own, made of ramps, tunnels, or anonymous avenues. Taking a taxi for a social reason, as I sometimes had to, I found it better to sit with my eyes shut. To ride in one looking out of the windows could undo whole days of patient work.

II

A LONG DAY

THE ONE THING WRONG with a Roman day is the break, the utter blank, in the middle—announced by the clanging down of black iron shutters, which before owners go off to lunch they stoop to lock. No place of business reopens till half past three or four. The effect on streets is a sudden dead-blinded look; or they seem like footways through a necropolis. Snuffed out are colours, glitter, and the desires played on by Rome's sensuous little shops—a desire which easily goes with no wish to buy. I avoided all but necessary shopping, and what becomes necessary is boring; therefore one should be able to get it

36

over in the most boring time of day, early afternoon. For me it was a matter of replacements: soap, shoes, flowers, writing paper, face powder, yet another copy of the Pianta, and so on. To be forced to lay in hosts of slippery parcels, and, still worse, go back with them to the hotel to be rid of them before going further, removes the bloom from a morning, the glow from a sunset. As things were, I was obliged to, and this riled me. Only in this particular did my ego come into collision with that of Rome.

I know it to be a civilized Latin custom, the siesta. An hour of stupor should not hurt one. But this is more than an hour; it not only lasts longer but goes deeper. Lessening traffic darts through the thoroughfares, as though before some impending disaster; on paralysed business buildings and aimless pavements there falls from the sky an unmeaning glare. It is not that nobody is about, but that those who are show themselves in a trauma, gait straggling or sagging and eyes vacant. Does this noonday midnight induce a sense of blanketing darkness, in which nothing is to be registered, nothing matters? In reality, secrets are exposed to one's eye, which begins to feel like a spy's camera. Once I saw a handsome, orthodox woman, in a street doorway next to a locked frontage, face and body convulsed by angry grief as though no one saw her. In Rome, where at all other times of day there is something measured even about fury, a niceness of degree in every extravagance, so

37

that no one seems totally off guard, these noon inadvertences loom large, to the point of seeming abnormal. Do people feel unseen when they cannot see themselves, as here at other hours they can and do? Glass, with mirror-panels set back behind it, duplicates everything going on in a Roman shopping street, which is thus lined by continuous moving friezes of reflections. These add, in themselves, a further dimension: only when shutters black out the glass does one realize how narrow the streets are. Without knowing, one has become accustomed to being accompanied by one's reflected self, the one figure with which one remains in step. Shorn of one's *Doppelgänger,* one is aware of something missing from one's identity.

This used to be the time when I lost my way even in the network round my hotel. For the closely similar yellow streets never were known to me by name: I had fallen into recognizing each by particular window displays and, no less, smells. But now, not only the eye is baffled but the nostrils: sealed completely away from one are the breaths from cheeses, artichokes moist from the garden, *marrons* moist from the syrup, candied fruits, sawdust, dusty nuts, oranges and apples, perfumed soap together with heated hairdressing, leather, gesso, spiced meats and fishy delicatessen, varnish, fresh flaky pastry and new bread, photographic accessories, freesias and hyacinths and jonquils, bales of textiles whether brocade or calico. Only eating-places, with slits of dark busy backs showing between immaculate curtains, or *espresso* bars with their leaden counters, are open: out trail the cooling-off fumes of meals, or, more energetic, wafts from the coffee being spurted into a thick cup.

Only the street-sweepers are themselves, come into their own, at work. My third day, confetti left from a rainy carnival was being dislodged from where it spattered and clung. Another day, I watched a tangle of cooked spaghetti, exposed on the ground on a piece of paper behind a stationary car, being swirled away from a cat which was settling down to it—the only Roman cat I ever saw thwarted. Lunging forward with their long-handled brushes, worrying stiff bristles into interstices, the sweepers advance in their flopping smocks down street after street, in armies of one. What a stay, what a comfort is their activity. And thanks to them Rome wakes, between three and four p.m., to a tail-end of afternoon pure as early morning. In season, they are followed by sluicing water carts. Only in village-like Trastevere do municipal sweepers not seem to operate. Trastevere, I was given to understand, owes much of its picturesqueness to its recalcitrance; it is for staying the way it was, and those who like that way like it very much. Coal dust, grit, waste paper, hen feathers are therefore shifted only by puffing winds; fruit rinds and dog dung stay undisturbed. For me,

Trastevere after nightfall, when you see no more than lamplight elects to show.

Till I learned how to live through it, the noon hiatus tired me like insomnia. Or I felt, when finally Rome banged open the shutters and launched into the second phase of activity, as though I, only I, had been up and about all night. This could not continue. Luncheon is after all the nominal reason for the pause: clearly a non-sleeper should eat longer. To sit down as late as hunger allowed, then spin the meal out and out was the answer. It was not so much a matter of consuming as of making last.

For the visitor, I began to see, it is more courteous to dawdle than to gobble—the restaurant comes to feel it has snared a *gourmet*, a meticulous chooser and slow savourer. The waiter is perfectly happy to drift away again, leaving one in conference with the menu—which, rendered ghostly by watered ink and mysterious by many abbreviations, is as lengthy as a reader could wish. There is a diversity to choose from, and if the diversity is almost the same as yesterday's at a similar restaurant, what matter? I always knew what I wanted, generally found it: all the more reason, therefore, not to appear to order at random or with an indifference due to haste, or, worst of all, haste due to indifference. In Rome only the nastiest restaurants—those serving warmed-over *pasta*, tinny *piselli*, withered *salami* to first-day tourists, who if they have sense do not come back again—are without pride; and even in one of those one may meet one proud waiter, whom one feels sorry for. The flourish and mutual flattery which can go on, while one is in the course of spinning a meal out, have both art and heart in them. No waiter hurries you; do not hurry him. Having set down your token basket of bread, he potters in figures of eight round his other tables, with extra solicitude for those empty, smoothing a cloth, cunningly changing the whereabouts of a salt cellar, or lifting a water carafe against the light as though to analyse its contents. Or he will pose for a minute or two in the street doorway. The restaurants I went to were middle-class; their prices varied as little as did their cooking. None were large; each held, besides about twenty tables, great hatstands branching in glossy commas. The chairs, whose perforated uncushioned seats were moulded to the average client's bottom, were as lovingly polished as the hatstands. There is sometimes an *art-nouveau* tiled dado, sometimes a modern mosaic floor, and there are never not proper napkins, however limp. The interior is drenched in thick creamy light from the curtains running across the window: the rail is about two thirds of the way up, and now and then there appears a pair of eyes looking in over it from the street side, either searching the restaurant for a friend or debating its gustatory possibilities.

A good eating-place, here as anywhere else, is to

be told by the type, number, and regularity of its patrons. A regular is, in turn, himself to be told by his way of casting his hat on to its comma and the taciturnity of his nod in response to greetings. Rubbing his hands together, he takes an inventory of the room before sitting down. Such patrons usually enter in twos or fours; one takes them to be confederates. Women are rare, unaccompanied women rarer—though to be one does not make one conspicuous. (Only two things in Rome, I found, make one conspicuous: one, failing to carry an umbrella when it rains, the other, sneezing—of which more later.) No same group appears by any means every day, each having several restaurants on its rota—nobody in Rome seems to like monotony, or to esteem persons they see too often, or be esteemed by persons who grow too sure of them. Noting this, I kept myself from any too marked addiction to any one restaurant, spacing out my appearances carefully—there is more *accueil* when one has not been seen for some time, though equally any too long absence makes for waning interest, due to one's infidelity. Sooner or later, I came to know each place's little bands of intermittent regulars by sight; and had, too, the interest of spotting them elsewhere. There may be a level exchange of glances; recognition, never familiarity.

Roman food of the kind to which I sat down is for the hungry, the healthy, and those in humour. As in

Rome I was seldom not all three, I have no other standards by which to judge it. Finer palates than mine find it unsubtle. At expensive places, to which I was taken for a treat, everything is too rich; one feels not exactly ill but subject to gastronomic boredom—eating at that level, the more pretentious, causes one to wish one were in Paris. (Again, altogether another thing is the cooking in most Roman private houses; the most delicious, I think, that I ever tasted.) The virtue of little-restaurant Roman food resides perhaps in consistency more than flavour—a matter of freshness, resilience, tenderness, and in the case of *pasta* sufficient slipperiness without oiliness. Vegetables, not numbed by a session in the refrigerator, come out of open air and from recent earth. All helpings are over-generous. I could not believe one could have enough *carciofi*, or green *tagliatelli*, or cuts of veal crisscrossed by marks from the grill, together with *insalata verde*, till experience taught me this could be possible. It becomes mortifying to watch the unflagging performance at other tables—when half the object of lunch is to spin it out, and when lavishly ordered it must be paid for, to be routed makes one look silly and feel chagrined. There is seldom, however, not room to conclude with oranges. A great ripe Sicilian blood orange is in a class by itself: the peel, mottled satin outside, white velvet in, curls away under digs from the thumbs, gladly; the delicate-membraned sections fall asunder like petals, firm flesh not spilling one drop of crimson juice till one bites into them. Such oranges deserve to be eaten as I ate them, in infiltrated sunshine, with wine to finish. You become invaded by the eupeptic mellowness of the atmosphere, blueing with cigarette smoke, and the trance over other tables not yet deserted. Now is the moment to send for coffee, to open but fail to read a history book, to unfurl but not study the Pianta—on which wine, orange, and coffee stains begin to write an over-map of their own. Hour of vision or of abeyance: who knows which? Something of both go out with one through the glass door.

After-lunch Rome looks like a stage set with the curtain up between it and an empty auditorium. And the walker walking when others sleep has the sense of being a sleepwalker. But waking purpose, within one, wakes one up. This is the hour of the impulse to break through this canvas simulacrum of a city into the reality at the other side of it: antiquity. Only the vestiges seem solid—Rome as it was underpropping Rome as it is. My steps headed themselves almost automatically, early afternoon after afternoon, towards one particular part of the open air.

The Forum, together with the Palatine, is open all day. No noon whistle sounds or shutters come down, cessation here being for always. "Now thy Forum roars no longer . . ." (Tennyson to Virgil).

Dregs of echoes have seeped down into the cracks in the sunken pavements; the ripple of excavations up the long valley is glacier-still, now and for evermore. The glare from above, so annulling elsewhere, falls here on nothing it can annul: rather, it gives void porticoes, unequal columns, sagging ascents of steps additional hardness, which becomes them. I like the Forum best at its most lucid and least shadowy—sunset, for instance, makes for distortions, also for an emotion which has no authorized place here. But now, in the stupefied afternoon, when the present seems to be at its lowest ebb and today's Rome ghostlier than yesterday's, is the right hour. Sit on a marble stump and take a long look round, before walking on.

What a pity one cannot enter the Forum from the Capitoline end, under the Arch of Severus: thus, one would face directly up the perspective. As it is, the one turnstile is on the flank; from it one pitches downhill on to the Via Sacra, midway in course. Each time, one requires two or three minutes to assemble oneself—to assemble the place takes longer. The Via Sacra, though to be thought of as the axis or spine of the Forum plan, runs anything but straight, and along one side, not the middle, of the flat-bottomed valley. Its meanderings among so many thought-out rectangles make it at once curious and natural.

The whole, as a whole, is best taken in from above

—by leaning over the parapet of the ledge roadway which, overhung by the Campidoglio, overhangs the Forum. True, one looks down into a pit or trough of which the foreground is too near up under the eye. But in the main it *is* when one sees from here that porticoes, ranks of columns, exposed ground-plans fall into the order of their relationship. For purely "viewing" the Forum, this is the viewpoint: still better (because one looks along, instead of across) than the lofty Farnese terraces on the Palatine. Probably one should contemplate, from the roadway, for longer than I, for one, am willing to do—it is not in nature not to want to get down *into* the thing, and as soon as possible. Could one only descend from here, without more fuss! The tedious way round to the turnstile is too long: in the course of it the Forum is lost to sight, and, worse, one's conception of it is lost also—how can one carry anything so far?

So one is plunged, keyless, in among the prostrate and the inchoate: lumps, pitfalls, discontinuous ridges. This might be an abandoned building-site, or outgrown giant playroom littered with breakages. Only the distance is noble with perpendiculars. The chaos into which the Forum was literally thrown exasperates (I learned) modern archaelogists, now in the course of putting it right—which involves pains they feel they should have been spared. Disarray was caused by the headiness, and the lack of method, of the original excavators—fired by the excitement of their patrons, those digging proceeded too fast apace. *Savants* who had inspired the enterprise failed, it now appears, to direct it calmly; the aristocratic enthusiasts who financed it fell prey to avid childish impatience. Everything dug up was flung about; which created, for the cooler heads to come later, needless exasperating enigmas. Today's reconstructions have been much hampered. What one finds (as by now even the layman knows) may be less important than where one finds it. Yesterday's *amateurs,* passionate for objects and swayed by drama, did not see in that light—and I cannot blame them. But for professionals, one must realize, it is as though poltergeists had got in first.

Work now going on on the Palatine is a model of temperance. The results are gigantic or pretty, always coherent. But the work *as* work is infernally slow to watch, bringing itself to inexplicable pauses for weeks together. More sympathetic, I find, that untutored frenzy which sent earth flying and scattered fragments of cornice, disjected inscriptions and limbs of statues piecemeal, unnumbered, from their unnoted beds. The history of the excavation of the Forum, though brief in comparison with its history proper, is no less fraught with battles of passion. Pilfering of marbles began before the ruins had quite submerged. The Renaissance Popes countenanced, here as elsewhere, sporadic digging; free-lance, therefore no doubt competitive. Trophies were carried off to adorn churches, palace galleries, villa gardens. In 1536, an attempt was made to lay bare the buried Via Sacra, in order that it should provide the course, and furnish associative glories, for the Emperor Charles V's triumphal procession—after that, it was left to silt up again. The grassy Campo Vaccino, overlaying the Forum, had (to judge by the old drawings) the hospitable, vague look of common land, grazed by cattle in transit, dotted with squatters' shacks. It undulated less like soil than like sand or snow, lapping unevenly up against façades or swallowing pediments completely, swelling up across arches—which, thus robbed of proportion, came to look like stunted monsters of breadth. Through the surface protruded remnants of porticoes. The gradations of ruin, one must remind oneself, are an affair of centuries—later-fallen columns lay across mounds which hid their fellows; lumps of masonry littered each other's graves. What remained in view has, in engravings and paintings, the air of tottering; so askew and unsteady appear the capitals, under the transverses they still support, that any moment of balance might be the final one. Uprights show gashes, like half-felled trees. One wonders at the unconcern of the lordly strollers, depicted gesticulating and pointing morals in the shadow of impending collapse. Their confidence was justified: nothing happened—the monuments were less precarious than they looked; or at any rate, than they looked to the artist. Here, for painter or draughts-man, was a searching subject: the Forum as an unconcluded battle between upstandingness and downfall—on which side was the beholder, each one in succession and each in turn, to throw his in its own way decisive weight? Did Claude, Van Heemserck, Canaletto, and others to whom we are indebted, perhaps exaggerate the unsafe? True, they show us nothing that could not be capable of re-maining standing; none of their stresses are at fault —yet Time, while we watch the picture, eats at the mortar; insidious trees' roots are thrusting the blocks apart; disintegration is in the colour of the atmosphere. These, the aesthetic records, remain our only ones. Gradually, with its graveyard out-lines, the place emerged from the apathy of the Dark Ages, the squalor of the Middle. A Giuseppe Vasi etching, 1765, shows it respectably flattened down, flanked by nice-looking houses on the Curia side, with an alley of trees planted down the centre —for an instant, one could feel sorry that such good order was on the eve of being disturbed. To other, less prosaic representations, allow an imaginative margin. Probably they are as dependable as most history, which, as it has come to be written down, represents also, largely, a way of seeing.

Making good, no less than digging out, played part in the reconstitution of the Forum. And the latest phase has been re-erection: whole fresh light crops of orderly pillars continue to spring up, almost overnight. . . . The delivery of the place, as a whole, from its load of earth began to be undertaken towards the end of the eighteenth century, and has, with pauses, gone on since then. The excited speed I envisaged cannot in reality have been possible: the displacement and shifting to elsewhere of tons of soil mingled with rubble, which had crushed pavements, borne down on masonry, choked foundations, must have been infinitely laborious. If the burial had not been deep, it was deep enough. The shattered, shamed, uncertain return to daylight—was it, after all, disappointing? There is a naïvety about the Forum as it now is. It is as though what is disinterred took on the character of the greater part of the time of its disinterring: the Palatine, later exposed, looks twentieth-century, the Forum, Victorian—still like a faint brown photograph in a rectory study.

Suppose the place *had* been left, undisturbed, for a hundred-and-fifty or so years more? Several generations would have been the poorer; and so, I think, would these incoherent vestiges themselves. Here in Antiquity's rock garden, among the thickets and aimless paths, edified wandering has gone on, ever since it was opened up to be wondered at. Ignorant people were enlarged by awe; for the educated there may have been something thwarting. For our sheltered forebears, there would have been something new in a wiped-out visage. Losing each other among the oleanders, poking with the ferrules of walking-sticks or parasols, skirting any pitfalls they saw in time, staring and exclaiming and misconstructing, they would come to stops, sit down on prostrate columns to rub twisted ankles or read aloud from Baedekers. They yawned, but not out of boredom, overcome by vague speculations and drifting fancies. And people, as though inadvertently making offerings, were for ever losing belongings in the Forum: pen-knives, diaries, handkerchiefs, bunches of seals. Brooches unpinned themselves and flashed down crevasses; single gloves lay perishing in the shaggy grass long after their owners had quitted Rome. The Forum leaves one with little to say to a companion: everything seems a platitude— in the distance one hears the hired accents of someone's guide, methodically rising and falling: the schoolroom sound has no place in this sleeping air. Yet there is a wordless echo of what the guide tells: the Forum voices itself to me in the afternoon, as it must have done to many before me—the desultory, the idle, the after-lunchers. There is eloquence in this extended dazzle of unearthed stone.

There is an alternative to lethargy: bestir yourself.

The point from which to start round the Forum is, I maintain, the Arch of Septimius Severus—under the Capitoline, in a corner. Standing with the Capitoline at your back, you have the length of the Forum stretched out before you. The book to carry is Miss Dorothy Robathan's *Monuments of Ancient Rome* (which is published in Rome and on sale at booksellers'). Keep your thumb in the book at Chapter iii; also unfold the map which is at the end: on this the monuments, each numbered, can be identified by the key in the margin.

You are facing down a lengthy oblong of space, down the left side of which runs a paved way. (Not the whole of this way is the Via Sacra; the Via Sacra breaks off from it, crosses the oblong then comes up towards you on your right.) All down the left of the oblong, over the paved way, large buildings were or are still aligned—the course I am proposing that you follow takes you past them, or their vestiges, one by one.

First comes the Curia, or Senate House. Its being set back somewhat, and at an angle from the rest of the frontage, is accounted for by its standing in the Comitium, a dedicated meeting-ground (see Miss Robathan) which adjoined but remained superior to the Forum. The Curia is not in ruins; it is roofed, has a high doorway, asks to be entered. Its dead-plain brick simplicity (like all else here, it has been stripped of marble) serves to bring out the virtue of its proportions—almost no other interior in Rome gave me such neutral but serene pleasure. The Senators' seating arrangements may be viewed, their procedure to an extent envisaged. It is hard to imagine anyone becoming excitable in this calm building. Now, in here, a number of carvings are being given shelter against the weather—among them, great processional marble panels which formerly decorated the Rostra. The original Curia, attributed to the third of the Kings of Rome, stood just to the west of the present site; its successor was begun by Julius Caesar in 45 B.C. and dedicated in 29 B.C. Additions were later made by Augustus. Little of uncle's or nephew's work is left, for Diocletian (Emperor A.D. 284–305) rebuilt the Curia during his reign.

Next, the Basilica Aemilia. This court of justice was the one building on this side of the Forum to be totally levelled to the ground. Till lately, therefore, Aemilia was represented by nothing but a respectfully blank space; now, token reconstruction is going on—the plan is outlined, vanished features suggested. (The neat line of houses shown by Giuseppe Vasi occupied, in its day, the Aemilia site.) The basilica dated back to 179 B.C.—traces of that epoch have been uncovered. It was rebuilt in 54 B.C., to remain as it was until 410 A.D., when it was set fire to by the Goths. The Emperor Honorius restored it, but final destruction remained in wait. . . . Sketched-in Aemilia has as upstanding neighbour the Temple of Antoninus and Faustina—a recognizable landmark, for its portico dominates almost every picture of the Forum. Antoninus Pius (Emperor from 138 to 161 A.D.) dedicated this to his wife Faustina during her lifetime; later the Empress, who survived him, caused the temple to sanctify both their names. Now, over the portico, with its enormous columns and flight of steps, shows the top of a church which niched itself into the ancient structure.

Next, a tree-darkened hollow: the Sepulchretum —a burying-place which predates the Forum of known history. Flanking on the necropolis is the circular Temple of Deified Romulus ("so called," qualifies Miss Robathan), whose beautiful verdigrised bronze door has the sad look of being sealed shut by dust. This building in 307 A.D. was dedicated to Romulus Augustus, son of the Emperor Maxentius. Behind and connecting with it is the church of SS. Cosmas and Damian, inserted into a portion of what was either the Temple of the Penates or the Library of the Temple of Peace, begun by Vespasian.

Next, the Basilica of Maxentius, with its raw tawny denuded brickwork, lofty broken vaultings, massive look of indignity. Halls with their fragments of coffered ceiling are torn open to daylight, their floors raised like stages above the Forum (and stages indeed they are, now, for summer concerts). Below them, a broken-off section of arcade remains from what was a grand entrance-way on the Via Sacra.

"The architectural features of this building are," Miss Robathan points out, "more like those of the imperial baths than those of other basilicas in the Forum." For this or whatever reason, the Maxentius basilica is what its Forum neighbours are not, at once melancholy and boring. It stands for broken purpose—begun during his reign (A.D. 306–312) by the Emperor who names it, it was re-planned convulsively by Constantine, when he had defeated Maxentius in the battle at the Milvian bridge. Shortly after his victory Constantine recognized Christianity. This basilica may be felt to conclude an epoch.

It is also the last building along this line. You have come, now, to the other end of the oblong—only to find yourself facing nothing particular. There is a vista, but you have the sensation that you ought not to be seeing down it. Beyond, a heaving view of the Colosseum. Between that and you, in the near foreground, perches Santa Francesca Romana, with its subtly simple Lombardi façade and its *campanile*. The church looks inadequate in the gap. In fact, the eminence raising Santa Francesca is a part of the platform which once supported the gigantic dual Temple of Rome and Venus. This, most spectacular building in the Forum, was at once the crown and terminal of the oblong. The portico (that is, at the "Rome" end) ran, with its peopled cascade of steps, ten Corinthian columns, imposing architrave, at a right-angle to the Maxentius frontage. To envisage it, in however ghostly a way, is to account for one's feeling of something missing.

The memorable twin temples stood back-to-back, that of Venus stopping just short of the Colosseum; to which *it* presented, also, a splendid face. There survives an apse with a wrecked ceiling, and there is a fair preservation of marble pavements. On the platform confronting the Colosseum, some of the forty-four granite columns have been set up again, those missing having as stand-ins columnar myrtle bushes—topiary art has added a myrtle staircase. (This promenade, airy as a deck, is outside the Forum.) Rome-and-Venus was begun by Hadrian, Emperor 117–138 A.D. The site it occupied had been that of a portion of Nero's Golden House: from somewhere about here rose, it is thought, Nero's ninety-five-foot statue of himself. Antoninus Pius, succeeding Hadrian, completed the work on Rome-and-Venus. When and in what manner the fall came, I do not know.

The Arch of Titus is to the right of the vanished temple—ground steadily rises towards it; it stands, in fact, at the highest point reached by the Via Sacra. Erected A.D. 81, by the Emperor Domitian, in honour of his deified brother Titus, the arch, eloquent with carvings, commemorates the sack of Jerusalem. Past it, you go no further.

Instead, face round the way you have come. Now, the far-off Capitoline makes a backdrop for the perspective down which you stare. On what has become your left, the immediate foreground is empty, grassy, anonymous: dints suggest diggings again filled in. This, which was the Forum's commercial quarter, held little of sacred or civic prestige. Pushed up against the haughty base of the Palatine, mushroom business houses and vice resorts fought one another for space, stamped each other down. Foundations and cellars came to form several strata—excavation, for instance, brought to light a brothel of Republican days from beneath a Neronian building of less clear purpose. Chaotic, competitive though it was, this area boasted an orderly frontage along the oblong—interrupted ridges, sunk in grass, remain from the *porticus margaritaria,* where pearl-sellers and jewellers had their shops. The luxury arcade faced across the Forum at the Basilica of Maxentius, opposite.

And this equivocal stretch had a chaste neighbour. For next comes the Atrium of the Vestal Virgins. In Rome's early days, the cult of Vesta concentrated close to the Via Sacra; but with time the sacred precincts expanded, till they ran back into the Palatine understructures. Still fairly modest under the Republic, they were taken in hand, enlarged, and redecorated by several Emperors—Nero, Domitian, Trajan, Septimius Severus. So many, thanks to Imperial enthusiasm, were the improvements (which more than once involved reorientation) that only a specialist can keep count of them. Enough to try to picture this pleasant place as it last was.

More or less, with Miss Robathan's aid, one can trace the plan. An open *peristyle* (court), with a colonnade, had on three sides rooms of varying sizes. The *peristyle* has today the look of a garden, touchingly if gruesomely set about with the heads, limbs, and portions of torsos of dismembered statues of famous Vestals. The mutilated company, one may hope, enjoys the feathery greenery, the flowerbeds, the sky-reflecting glitter of three tanks, sunken, marble, brimming with water. The octagonal pattern in the middle is enigmatic: was it, as some suppose, the base of a summerhouse? At one end, the *peristyle* is raised: steps lead up, from a coloured pavement, to a landing off which open six rooms—these, it is assumed, were the studies or offices of the six Vestals. If so, they fared better by day than night: it is to be feared they slept at the back, in the dank apartments overhung by the Palatine. Sunlessness, however, was mitigated by a heating system, whose workings you may examine. Off that same corridor were the kitchens: two ovens and a small mill are to be found. The existence, as a whole, of the Vestal Virgins fascinates me; later I must say more of it.

A segment of the circular Temple of Vesta, in which the Vestal-tended fire was kept burning, stands near the Atrium, at the Capitoline end—too white, it looks what it is: lately reconstructed. Not far away, and far more delightful, is the Spring of Juturna (a water nymph), most ancient spring in the Forum. The lip of the wellhead is grooved by use; overlooking the basin a carved altar shows Castor and Pollux (who watered their horses here), Jupiter, Leda and the Swan, and their daughter Helen garbed as goddess of light. Pretty (as is no other thing around you), the spring is a sort of oasis, where you may rest.

In line with Juturna but some way out into the open oblong, look for the travertine foundations of the now vanished triple Arch of Augustus, erected 29 B.C. This, in its day, flanked the Temple of Deified Julius—dedicated the same year as the arch went up. The temple, also built by Augustus, stood plumb in the middle of the Forum, thereby blocking the view from end to end. No tribute to an assassinated uncle can have been ever more unignorably placed. Augustus had authority for the site: the temple rose over the spot—marked by an altar—where Julius Caesar's honoured, dagger-hacked body (*"thou bleeding piece of earth"*) had been burned ceremonially by the populace swayed by Mark Antony's oration. The temple was vowed by the Triumvirs two years later, that is, 42 B.C. By all accounts it was noble, ample, and simple; it faced towards the Capitoline. Nothing of it is left but the frontal platform, which lately has been restored.

Close behind Deified Julius is a hillock of massive

fragments, once the Regia. Tradition ascribes the Regia's founding to Numa, second King of Rome: the debris we see represents the work of Augustus, who gave the early record house final form. The Regia is not difficult to locate, being exactly across the way from the Antoninus-Faustina portico.

Leaving the middle of the oblong, return to the Spring of Juturna. Above this soars yet another landmark, lovely and unmistakable—the three Corinthian columns which, still supporting a section of their entablature, survive from the otherwise-fallen Temple of Castor. The temple, founded *circa* 484 B.C., had origin in the Castor-and-Pollux legend. It owed its final embodiment to Tiberius. The trio of uprights, with crosspiece, has twice over a dreamlike familiarity; not only does it appear in all Forum paintings but it looks like a giant petrified cricket wicket.

Next to the vacant floor-space of the Temple of Castor is, or was, the Basilica Julia. (The Via Sacra, by now having crossed the oblong, proceeds past it.) The two-storeyed pillared and galleried hall of justice used, when it stood, to look across at its sister basilica, Aemilia. Founded by Julius Caesar, in 54 B.C., it was rebuilt three times, ever more ostentatiously, by the Emperors Augustus, Carinus, and Diocletian. A.D. 305 saw the final version. It perished slowly; its ruins suffered the white-ant activities of the Middle Ages, the yield of marbles here being extra rich. What remained after the robbing was calcinated. One "enters" the Basilica Julia, today, depressingly easily, simply by stepping up on to the bedrock of its lost pavement. Lately, some columns have been returned to it.

The Temple of Saturn, next door, might seem by contrast all but intact—nothing in fact does survive but the noble portico's unbroken row of Ionic columns. With these, you reach the Capitoline head of the valley: this is the point where the Forum is cut across, overhung, by the embankment and parapet of the modern roadway. Above the road, niched against the Capitoline and, thus, facing down the perspective I call the oblong, are considerable vestiges of three buildings: the Porticus Deorum Consentium (a deity-statued colonnade past which the Clivus Capitolinus went up from the Forum to the Temple of Jupiter), the Temple of Vespasian (begun by the Emperor's sons, Titus and Domitian, in 79 A.D.), and the Temple of Concord. Concord first came into being, 366 B.C., to celebrate the official end of the struggle between Rome's patricians and plebeians. What is left of it dates, again, from Tiberius.

The above three buildings, at their high level, strike one as exiles from the rest of the Forum. This is a wrong impression: they belong to it—having formed part of the unbroken architectural ascent crowned by the vast, flat-topped Tabularium.

Brought to a halt by the parapet, you look up at the viewpoint from which you once looked down. To your right (now) is the Arch of Septimius Severus —you are more or less back where you started from, without, yet, having by any means seen all. For instance, directly in front of you (in the centre, at the head of the oblong) is the Rostra—or at least, its foundations, from which you must reconstruct. This was the balustraded platform from which political speakers addressed the people: it took its name from the "beaks" of captured ships, with which it was decorated at first—later, the trophies were simulated in bronze. Originally the Rostra was in the Comitium; it was moved to its present position (less sacred but more commanding) by Julius Caesar. Augustus enlarged and adorned it; Septimius Severus carried out alterations, at the same time flanking it with his arch. The Rostra, up to the time of its collapse, was panelled with splendid marble reliefs, scenes from Rome's triumphs (those now placed for shelter inside the Curia).

Up in the rough grass bank behind the Rostra are two stumps. The first, cylindrical brickwork once cased in marble, is the Umbilicus: thus was marked the centre or navel of the City of Rome. The second is what remains of the once glittering Milliarium Aureum, pillar on which Augustus caused to be engraved, in gold, the distance from Rome of each of the principal cities of the Empire. There stood on top of this a symbolic figure, casting out darts—north, south, east, west: the roads.

Descend from the bank; face the other way. In line with the Rostra, a little way down the oblong, rises the very tall column of Phocas, fluted white marble—once it supported a statue in gilt bronze. The column was a late-comer to the Forum; in fact the last of the monuments here set up. It was erected by Smaragdus, Byzantine King of Italy, as far on as 608 A.D.; in style it pre-dates its inscription by several centuries—the monarch probably ravished it from elsewhere. Spaced down, also, along the oblong are what are taken to be the sites of two famed equestrian statues: the Emperors Domitian and Constantine. (Domitian's suffered the damning fate of everything connected with his memory.)

If I come, at this point, to an exhausted stop, it is not because the Forum has been exhausted. My account must clearly be incomplete, but I do not believe it to be misleading—these things *are* where I have said them to be. My route, I have so far found, does not correspond with any recommended by an authority—can this mean, simply, that it has not been thought of? Mine corresponds with my sense of order: the taking of things as one comes to them, one by one, placing them by their relation to one another. My approach to the Forum was visual rather than historic—even though "seeing," the greater part of the time, had to be an act of the mind's eye

63

(or better, that of directed imagination). To re-create, even for an instant, what is laid low, dishev-elled, or altogether gone into thin air is exciting. The study of anything that has disappeared is a call on faith. What is totally vanished raises peculiar ques-tions—out of a number of haughty buildings re-duced to the equalitarianism of being nothing, to which is one to give precedence, in recalling them? Why have I dwelled upon the Rome-and-Venus tem-ple, and not more than named the Golden House? Answer, in this case—the Golden House is in itself a subject, to be returned to.

I kept to my route, many afternoons, in deferen-tial defiance of Miss Robathan, who advocates an in-structed zigzagging. Her route is the specialist's, mine the country cousin's. It may be noted that, in giving directions, I have altogether cut out points of the compass; for the reason that I am never sure of them—"slightly to the north of" or "two or three paces to the south-west" involves me in infinite extra thought. "Left" and "right" seem foolproof; pro-vided you know, as I did, which way you are at the moment looking. In my account of the Forum there must be oversights: I speak of ruins or remnants I came to know, omitting—naturally—those in regard to which I had some incurable blind spot, distaste, stupidity, or laziness. I do not, however, think I have by-passed anything important. The shreds of infor-mation I relay come from worthy guide-books, in which the rest is to be found. One is miserable in the Forum without a guide-book; yet, when one has one, unevenly receptive to what it says. Of the totality of facts and findings, some few seize upon one, others flee by. Or so I found. What I have noted is what, for me, threw most light on what there was to be seen. I was grateful for anything that could serve to pin down at least some part of the broken pattern.

Dates. I like these because they provide framework. They are plain information of the first order. I wanted to establish the Forum monuments' nearness to or distance from one another in time as well as in space. Clearly some are the seniors, other the juniors. Many of them were one another's contemporaries—for how long, and when, did they share the same term of time? Of these temples, courts of justice, government buildings, memorials, archive libraries, sacred places of abode, how many supplanted others? The Imperial arches, lofty solitary columns, mounted statues, dedicated altars were works of egotism or pious memory—what fed the egotism or inspired the memory? Which, and above all when, were the victories, martial or civic, and/or the noble deaths thus recalled? *Something* is, was, stated, boasted of, or lamented everywhere in this full, small space of the Forum: the place would be a welter without chronology. I attach dates to most of the monuments because it was through those, partially, that they spoke to me. They themselves I give

in the order in which I saw them—one by one, in the
course of walks: down one side of the Forum, turn
at the far end, then up the other.

All said and done, why re-evoke the Forum?—
why should my senses wish to do so? As it was, it
would have been insupportable: heatedness, glare,
clamour beating like so many gongs on the brain.
When the overhanging buildings, all day sunstruck,
sent up a quiver dulled by ascending dust to a copper
haze; or when wind howled through the porticoes,
having to be out-shouted, whipping rain aslant into
foul brown puddles—who could wish to be there?
Tension wired the air of this hemmed-in valley, by
physical nature torpid, staled by sweat, exhausted by
lungs. And to the overcrowding, surging and shov-
ing living and breathing humans on the outdoor floor
was added a population of statues, at every eminence
—topping columns, looking out in rows from the
arcaded windows of upper storeys, or lined up along
the parapets of roofs. Some gesticulated, others
struck athletic or martial attitudes, others, arms
folded, remained in a blind sternness of which the
meaning must have worn off. Over that theatre of
the mortal passions these stood for the only immortality to be hoped for. Nor were they all: on the tops
of arches for ever pranced teams of ferocious horses;
others snorted beneath Imperial riders. To human
and animal agitation was added a flapping of gilded

66

wings by sub-divinities and extended eagles. High
points of bronze, gilded bronze, or actual gold shot
forth ostentatious rays where the sun caught them,
among the glossy monotony of marbles. Work on
one building if not another being almost continually
in progress, there can seldom not have been scaffolding in the Forum, together with heaving, haul-
ing, and hammering.

The architecture sponsored by the Forum repro-
duces itself sadly elsewhere, today. From the Roman
idea have spawned endless civic buildings: town
halls, terminal railway stations, banks, exchanges,
middle-aged universities, museums, art galleries,
public libraries, secular-looking churches, and so
on. Grime-caked and smoke-darkened in northern
cities, these reproductions bear down crushingly
on the spirit, alienating one from the benefits they
stand for—solidarity and probity, culture, philan-
thropy, the reliability of transport, the respectability
of God. Nobody elbowing their way past them in
sooty rain, or unwillingly entering their portals, or
glancing up into their fog-filled vaultings, could fail
to be prejudiced against things Roman. Someone I
met in Rome told me how he had the pleasure of
motoring into it with a friend who had refused to
come here before. "Why," exclaimed the friend,
looking round, "it's yellow! I had expected everything to be *dark grey*." The Forum was never that:
on the contrary, pale- or bright-coloured marble

facings enhanced daylight. Recollect also, classic architecture is in origin and conception Mediterranean: it expects to be slotted by sky-blueness, honeyed by sunshine, able to cast shadows in whose sharpness there is something transparent. In its proper air it does not look overweight. Also, its epoch was pre-industrial—it suffers in densened atmospheres, under murky skies. (As against that, it suits almost any landscape, particularly the wooded, watery, or hilly: nothing seems wrong with a porticoed country house or a *tempietto* in a moist northern garden.)

Noise. The roar of the Forum must have arisen largely from human shouting. The acoustics, the multiplicity of resoundings, if not echoes, are hard to imagine now the buildings are gone. If decorum reigned (largely) inside the Curia, in the Vestals' precincts, and within temples, restraint was thrown to the winds outdoors. Much was being demonstrated and marketed simultaneously; politics and commerce accounted for bellowings and mutterings; rumors tore through like speed-boats, leaving a wake; scandals were mongered at top market; intrigues drew together excited knots. Makeshift shops were pockets of screaming bargaining. The attraction of the Forum for otherwise supercilious persons, such as men of letters, was that *something* was always afoot, always going on. "What's new?"—the answer was in the Forum. The place set up an itch

68

which one had to satisfy—therefore no day, for an intelligent Roman, was complete without a quick dip into the *mêlée*. Poets who retreated to the country congratulated themselves on being at a distance from the Forum (it seems to me) almost ostentatiously. Clip-clop of plebeian ill-fitting sandals, up and down steps and across pavements, would have also added considerably to the din.

That, though enough, was all. There was no wheeled traffic—other than the chariot of a notability or a civil servant dashing through on priority business, or the privileged carriages of the Vestal Virgins. The oblong had in its middle a smooth-paved rectangle, dotted with statues, diagonally crossed by the Via Sacra and edged by other rough-surfaced thoroughfares. It tilted up at each end; the centre was flat. The centre sustained a stare from arcades of basilicas, elevated frontages of temples, and the distance-framing triumphal arches—these last all faced either up or down it.

The greatest change between then and now (other than the elimination of buildings) is in the backdrop to the Forum's perspective, the Capitoline. When a Roman, once, looked up at this from below, he saw something of an entirely different outline. He beheld the Capitol, which today's hill supported. That, though another chapter, must here be spoken of as a scenic accessory to the Forum. The hill had a trough in the middle; nothing appeared above the flat, statued top of the Tabularium. The trough was, however, between two spurs: on the southern (your left, as you face the hill) rose the Temple of Jupiter, superb on its sky-high, staircased, built-up platform. On the northern, set back further but likewise high, stood the Temple of Juno Moneta. From a distance, to a shortsighted Roman, the Capitoline must have looked like a stag's skull with rising antlers.

Today, the height-accent is in the centre: the *campanile* of the Palazzo Senatorio (begun at the end of the Middle Ages). The Palazzo is superimposed on the Tabularium—ancient-Roman arcades, with three arches open, appear under the early-Renaissance windows. The effect is, of a façade forming a cliff—this is one of Rome's outstanding examples of architected, therefore non-natural, height. By contrast, there is a falling-away at one side, that on which once soared the Temple of Jupiter. (The temple is nowhere; its site is a public garden, airy and with a great Roman view.) On the other side, the decline is less, Juno's temple being replaced in altitude by the church of Santa Maria in Ara Coeli. And over the top of Santa Maria's roof glistens the topmost tier, the white-sugar summit of the Vittorio Emanuele Monument (begun 1885, inaugurated 1911: based, as we know, in the Piazza di Venezia and known to some as "the wedding cake"). On that summit, what? Teams of ferocious horses, charioteered by divinities who flap wings.

* * *

People I met in Rome legitimately wanted to know what I was doing.—Writing something?—Not while I was here.—No, really?—Pity to stay indoors.—Sight-seeing, simply?—Partly.—Ah, gathering background for a novel to be set in Rome!—No.—No? Look at Henry James.—Yes.—Then a travel book: where was I going next?—I was staying here.—Then, something in the way of a gay guide-book?—I was afraid I should be no help to anyone else.—Then it would have to be a book of impressions: but why Rome?—What was the matter with Rome?—It was not Greece.—I supposed not. —Did I, for instance, for an instant imagine that Rome was old?—It was not too old.—Not too old for what?—Me.—Then I did not care for antiquity? —Not in the abstract.—What did I see in Rome, then?—Beginning of today.—That made today long!—Today is being a long day.

But what did I like about Rome?— It was substantial.—And?—Agreeable.—Once, or now?—Altogether.—Agreeable was hardly the word for history.—Then there must be something in spite of that.—Well, I should not find I got far with the ancient Romans.—No?—No, they would not appeal to me.—Why not, specially?—They were unimaginative.—They were, were they?—Yes, most antipathetic.—I was not looking for friends.

I must look out, or Rome would ruin my style.

Oh?

Oh, yes! Attempts to write about Rome made

writers rhetorical, platitudinous, abstract, ornate, theoretical, polysyllabic, pompous, furious.

Had this been so in all cases?

Too many.

Language seldom fails quietly, it fails noisily.

So went several conversations, or interrogatories. Curiosity in Rome is a form of courtesy. The questions were disconcerting in being too much to the point, to the point too soon. I was never ready for them; accordingly I may well have sounded recalcitrant, "clever," or plain stupid. I had nothing to hide, but also little to show. I could not say what I intended doing, for that was not yet known to myself; at the most I had a notion or suspicion, such as one might form with regard to somebody else if one were to watch their movements hourly, closely. Shyness, involved in any affair of feeling, made me unforthcoming; also I never shook off my fear of presumption in having "designs" on Rome, of whatever kind. The idea of putting Rome into a novel not only did not attract me, it shocked me—*background*, for heaven's sake! The thing was a major character, out of scale with any fictitious cast. Other novelists had not felt this, and evidently (where they were concerned) rightly; their books were triumphs —if triumphs, also, over difficulties they had not had. For me, there was point-blank impossibility; not because I did not believe in art but because I did. There are two kinds of reality, which are incompatibles. Here in Rome as a spectacle was the story, and enough. Contained, it was to be picked up fragmentarily, humbly, inevitably in my case dimly and at heaven knew how many removes—or still more at which points and in what order. The omissions probably would be the most telling. The fabric, tattered away in parts, was people's existences and their doings.

Troubling as it was to be asked questions, it led to my putting them to myself. Omnivorous drifting cannot go on for ever; one cannot continue to take in everything for the sake of nothing. Each conversation left me with racing thoughts; after each, my rapid excited monologue, in beat with my excited solitary walking, took up again—and from a point further on. Often it took the character of an argument. I had noted, it had been borne in on me, that my loverlike ambiguous taste for Rome roused opposition; I seemed to be called upon to defend it. Rome in some roundabout way was not quite approved of. Deprecation—that was the attitude, on the whole. Naturally, that hardened me in my course.—What my course was, I should discover from where it took me.

Looking in Rome for characters other than the city, I began by heading for those magnified by history, favourably or not. I began with the Emperors. These appeared to divide themselves, with regard to Rome, into makers and unmakers; a division which held good, looking further back, with out-standing figures of the Republic. Was it less true of millions who had blown away on the dust—can *any* person live and have no effect? Negativity, if there be any, is a form of destruction. Simply, to be a Somebody (that is, of position) involves more: it may not matter more but it counts for more. No wonder drama took for its figures kings, made the court the prototype of society; and no wonder history has learned from drama—persons not dramatizable are not recorded; they do not go for nothing but must appear to. . . . Then again in Rome there had been the host of those represented by portrait busts, now in museums, labelled "unknown," or by just-legible names on outlying tombs—the suffi-ciently affluent and perhaps respectable. Below them, gradations of anonymity (with here or there a case of talent or scandal) down to mass-level. The Roman masses, I got the impression, sim-mered, sometimes just off boiling-point, placated by free entertainment, brutalizing in nature, and grants of wheat. Against hardship, balance some of the pleasure inherent in being alive at all! "Average" existences, at whatever level, are probably the hard-est to conceive of, when they are other than one's own. One of the merits of the Palatine, as a start, was its demarcation by individuals. There was no such thing as an "average" Roman Emperor.

* * *

74

On the Forum side, the built-up Hill of the Caesars looks like a giant derelict hotel: a honeycomb
of arches of keyhole narrowness, cavernous windows, gloomy vaulted apartments, ramps, and galleries. The overhangingness and the staringness are
unnerving. Sense of place and of a further dimension
begins on the plateau at the top—or rather plateaux,
for the levels are many. Here and there, also,
grasslands tumble and spill downhill. Up-and-down
winding walks and wooded hollows contrast with
pavements splintered but formal. The Palatine as I
found it in February seems still to be under the spell
of mild late autumn. Birds utter solitary unmating
notes; dusk emanates, any time of day, from humid
underground corridors and successions of cavities
without echoes. Now, out of season, there are few
visitors; the custodians, wrapped in greatcoats and
their own thoughts, interfere with nothing that is not
forced upon their notice. Willing to act as guides,
they are content not to. Out of their view, unde-
terred, one may penetrate past tangles of rusted
wire into slippery understructures half-choked by
rubble, or out on to heights barred by warnings:
pericoloso. On the time-shorn Palatine, little rises
above one: one assesses height, rather, by looking
down, into the far-below vacant world of excavated
series of halls of pleasure. The hill seems so riddled
hollow, one asks oneself why it does not collapse. It
seems most itself at an early-springtime six o'clock

75

in the evening, when to its atmosphere of evapo-
rated pomp and residual danger is added one's risk
of being locked in. How far it would be an ordeal
to be there alone for a night, I was never certain:
the draughty dark would be troubled by crepitations
from the iron sheeting over the diggings, or the desiccated rustle of wintry ilexes; but the Palatine has
not soul enough to be haunted. However, I was not
put to the test. Veteran residents of Rome walk their
dogs on the Palatine around sunset, and their calcu-
lation of time, down to the last possible of the dark-
ening seconds, is infallible. They are the clocks to
watch; when at last *they* turn to the gates, one is
wise to follow.

The Palatine has a peculiar daylight, in which its
shabby subtle colours appear. Here and there the
black in the heaving pavements is more blotted out
than the salmon pinks. And daylight is to be recommended for the taking of one particular way up, not
generally used and I think rewarding. You *can* ascend, from the Forum, either by the Clivus Palatinus
(the former Imperial route, still paved, now flanked
by a convent wall and shady and naïve as a country
lane) or by letting the steps at the back of the
Atrium of the Vestal Virgins conduct you into the
upward zigzag of ramps and vaultings. But try, too,
keeping round the base of the hill, at the Capitoline
end, along under the wall of the Via di San Teodoro
—past the butt end of the church, small locked

76

gardeners' sheds, and compost heaps of last year's scythed weeds and grass. This brings you out over the Circus Maximus. Here, where it looks across at the Aventine, over the trough of the Circus, the Palatine is unkempt and steep, and across the face of the slope there run many dog-paths. Thin thorn-bushes, which flower sparsely and early, clutch at the soil between bosses of glossy serrated leaves—the architectural acanthus, more familiar to many when cut in stone. Foothold on any of the dog-paths is worth maintaining: you are taken along under the whole immense rampart-like frontage: porches launched into air, windows wide as gates. Finally comes the Septimius Severus structure's two-floored arcade and plum-coloured inner darkness—the lower passage, resembling some eerie subway of a moribund London railway station, must be followed: this has become your way from the outside into the inside of the Palatine. The sky once more, at the top, is like that of heaven.

The Palatine has been called the Cradle of Rome. Though from it, later, came the word "palace," there is something rebellious about its contours—legend, the primitive mysticism of the birth-place, outlives the succeeding tawdry story. Here, it is held, Romulus founded the original Rome; here were established the forefathers; here, stone by stone, came into being the fortified city of the Kings, altars dedicated to the protecting gods, who had not yet turned away their faces. Hymns rose from the templed corners of this island-like hill, coming to be answered, as time went on, by singers and lyres on the Aventine. Though the Palatine as it now is does not seem haunted, as it once was it had the power to haunt. Throughout the Rome that was to come to be ran the anguish set up by forfeited innocence, lost inspiration, corrupted purpose. Ruthless battles, predatoriness, everything that is harsh about an implanting, characterized those early days—which nevertheless assumed an undying light for the days after. The idea of redemption, with its power to fire, recurs throughout the history of Rome.

The Republic, in its turn to survive as a moral memory, saw the growth of Rome out on to other hills. The Palatine then became residential, sought by the eminent. Quiet with gardens, sanctified by their origin, these heights were favourable to the private hours of public figures and to the reflections of those who spoke to be heard. Cicero, Hortensius, Crassus, Catiline made their homes here; and it was, I suppose, such associations which first drew to the Palatine Octavius, Julius Caesar's great-nephew, who became Augustus when he was Caesar also. Alas, his choice brought no good to the hill, for on to it his dreadful successors followed him. Augustus himself lived on the Palatine with a well-known simplicity. Livia, whom he had desired, was his wife; she gave stylish enchantment to their modest surroundings. To her we owe the small sequence of painted rooms, lyrical, on two sides of a sunken courtyard—to enter the House of Livia is to yield to it. It is near the square mound, topped by the grove of ilex, which once was the Temple of Cybele, Magner Mater.

Up a staircase, in an eyrie-like study, the man of the new world worked at increasing pressure. The stages by which he arrived at being Augustus should be noted—there is no option as to Augustus: one *must* read history. It would appear that he did not (or at any rate acted as though he did not) ever wholly envisage becoming what he became, till he had become it. The mantle devolved upon him; the very mantle which Julius, his great-uncle, had been struck down for devising. His seems an outstanding one of those Roman destinies in which there was an element of compulsion, of non-alternative. One thinks more of pressures when they force a man towards doom; one forgets there are pressures towards glory. To a point, circumstances constructed the first Emperor, but they worked upon a man in himself constructive. Augustus was what it became essential for him to be. To study his face in marble is to wonder how far the portrait was idealized: one can only say that such a face would be likely for such a man. Not inspired, it would be likely to inspire. Reflectiveness, balance, and resolution are unmarred by the jutting or bloating of feature nowadays sometimes miscalled "strength." There is something touching, imperfect, about magnitude. This sonless man set his hopes on heir after heir; each in turn was snatched from him, young, by death. If any one of those youthful bright ones *had* lived, how would he have prospered? Finally, there was no one left but Tiberius, the embittered stepson, in whom years of disfavour had turned the soul sick.

Augustus founded the line of Caesars known as the Julio-Claudian. With the last of them there expired (and none too soon) the idea of lineal descendancy—of there being, *per se,* an imperial stock. "The hereditary principle, which," says Samuel Dill, "had been grafted on the principate of Augustus . . . inflicted on the world a succession of fools and monsters. The only hope lay in elevating the standard of virtue, and in the choice of a worthy successor by the form of adoption." The change was accomplished, but not before Caesarship had acquired a bad name; nor was there immediate improvement. Out of twelve who followed upon Augustus, seven died by violence. Their existences were nervous and ostentatious. They encaged the Palatine in marble, over which ran blood, more than once their own. The role impossible to fill was dangerous in its appeal to manias: man after man tottered under the idea of godship—since the Emperor was *a* god, why not God?—inflicting the terrors that they felt. The "why" of excesses must be deficiency.

AUGUSTUS (reigning, 27 B.C.–14 A.D.) had been the son of the daughter of Julius Caesar's sister, Julia: his father was M. Claudius Marcellus. TIBERIUS (14–37) was the elder of Livia's two sons by her first marriage to T. Claudius Nero. Gaius, better known as CALIGULA (37–41), was Augustus's great-grandson, in this manner—Augustus had had by *his* first marriage, to Scribonia, a daughter named Julia: Julia's second daughter, Agrippina the Elder, married the general Germanicus and bore, among better children, Gaius-Caligula. CLAUDIUS (41–54) was Caligula's uncle, having been the un-illustrious younger brother of Germanicus. Germanicus and Claudius had had as father Drusus the Elder, Livia's second son by her first marriage: the brothers thus were nephews of Tiberius; in addition to which their mother, Antonia Minor, had been the second daughter of Mark Antony and his wife Octavia, Julius Caesar's niece. This was the same Octavia whose first marriage (to M. Claudius Marcellus) had made her the mother of Augustus: Claudius was thus half-brother to Augustus. NERO (54–68) was at once Claudius's stepson and great-nephew—Claudius having taken as second wife (after the liquidation of Messalina) his niece Agrippina the Younger. She, daughter of Agrippina the Elder and

81

Germanicus, thus had been a sister of Caligula's. Agrippina the Younger's first husband, father of Nero, had been Cn Domitius Ahenobarbus—son of Antonia Major, the elder daughter of Mark Antony and Octavia. Nero's grandmother, on the paternal side, had thus been half-sister to Augustus.

Agrippina the Younger murdered Claudius, her uncle-husband, in order that Nero might succeed him. She exhausted, by her subsequent interfering-ness, any such gratitude as her son felt, and he had her murdered some years later. Nero's enforced death brings to an end your, or my, need further to struggle to disentangle the blood-relationships between the Julio-Claudians—on which I may seem to have dwelt with perverse pleasure. I am Irish, and interested in "family" and the complexities wrought by intermarriages. Those who are not may dismiss the foregoing paragraph, which all the same I do hope is clear.

Confusion, other than genealogical, followed upon the horrible death of Nero. 68 A.D. came to be known as "the year of the four Emperors"—the aspirants rapidly swept away being GALBA, OTHO, and VITELLIUS. In principle, it is to be borne in mind, an Emperor was the apex of a triangle whose other points were the Senate and the Army. He was where he was, and what he was, by virtue of the consent of the former, the support of the latter. It had so happened that the legionaries by elevating Augustus had instated a constitutionalist of the first order; but for too long this was not to occur again. Under his successors, conflict between the Palatine and the Curia became, if not continuous, continual; and not less recurrent were threats of military dictatorship. The post-Nero chaos was ended by the establishment of the Flavian Emperors—VESPASIAN (69–79), TITUS (79–81), and DOMITIAN (81–96). After the Flavians had run their course came NERVA (96–98), TRAJAN (98–117), then HADRIAN (117–138). Hadrian was followed by the Antonine Emperors—ANTONINUS PIUS (138–161), MARCUS AURELIUS (161–180), and COMMODUS (180–192). Then, after a dislocation and again chaos, came SEPTIMIUS SEVERUS (193–211). At this point I think I may pause.

Though I love to walk about on the Palatine, there is something exhausting, because exhausted, about the place, which may cause a sudden fatigue of body. I often found myself sitting on the ground (for there is nothing else there, often, to sit on) and each time I thought of King Richard II. The Emperors were not Shakespearean characters; not even Shakespeare could have made them so. Yet, they were designated chief actors, spotlit up to the moments of their dooms. The imperial predicament, as they knew it, had something in common with the royal. Their awfulness was the pollution of a tragedy; but there *was* a tragedy, somewhere, to be polluted.

> For God's sake, let us sit upon the ground
> And tell sad stories of the death of kings:
> How some have been depos'd, some slain in
> war,
> Some haunted by the ghosts they have
> depos'd,
> Some poison'd by their wives, some sleeping
> kill'd;
> All murder'd: for within the hollow crown
> That rounds the mortal temples of a king
> Keeps Death his court, and there the antick
> sits,
> Scoffing his state and grinning at his pomp,
> Allowing him a breath, a little scene,
> To monarchize, be fear'd, and kill with looks,
> Infusing him with self and vain conceit,
> As if this flesh which walls about our life
> Were brass impregnable; and humour'd thus
> Comes at the last, and with a little pin
> Bores through his castle wall, and farewell
> king!

And there the antick sat. . . . The Roman Empire, as an empire, was most personally tragic, within its first hundred years, because of a line of figures who were distorted. After that, one must not forget, there sat in improvement, a continuous steadying on the destined course. The age of the Antonine Emperors was to be marked by humane, conscientious rule. One must be on guard against misconceptions, when trying to grasp the movement of the history of Rome—untruths are thieves, robbing us of a birthright. One fallacy (promulgated I can't think how, though there are times when I see why) is that Rome's becoming an empire was the first step on the way to decline and fall. On the contrary: when the Republic ceased to be effectual, Rome's greatest achievements still were lying ahead. One must not fail to distinguish between the Empire and the Emperors: the former proceeded, functioning and thriving, while the latter, often, were at their most disastrous. An organism may have a generic strength which defends it against the power of persons. Conspicuously, the early Caesars offered examples of what was worst to those of unbending mind, implacable spirit, who were lamentors of the Republic. Unmitigatedly this was a bad start—but may not a bad start be possibly less demoralizing than a bad ending, petering-out confidence? For worse or better, the Republic was a thing of the past. The instated Empire required a new form of thinking, concept of action: in the main those who were capable were the governors—between whom and the new-rich satellites of the Palatine there was a savingly wide gulf. One dare not, all the same, minimize reigns of terror: the Republic had been aristocratic; the early Caesars altered the social landscape by exterminating or breaking the nobler families, as one might fell trees. Yet there were other times when they did no worse than give themselves over to wickedness in a vacuum. Suspiciousness was among the maladies from which they suffered; in this they resembled the common people—with whom, as was to be seen, they had tastes in common, and who possibly would have behaved much as did the Caesars had they felt free to and had the money. Surprisingly seldom do those showy neurotics seem to have been objected to by the populace, whom they not only entertained but made news for. Would we, ourselves, honestly, wish the Caesars to be missing from history? The Palatine, though burdened with hated memories, has shattered itself into the hill of Rome which is most lovely, consuming by its silence all those enormities. The ruins have been weathered and washed to all but innocence.

I re-live an afternoon of more than twenty years ago, when so much of the Palatine had not yet been excavated and stretches of it were bedded with blue irises. It was April. The idle yet intense air smelled of honey; Rome shimmered below with hardly a stir, and bluer than the sky were the Alban hills. There was a harmony between the distances. I was sitting on a broken ridge, reading and sometimes not reading a book. Low but clear voices, coming across the irises, told me that a couple who had been wandering had set down behind me—students, by their serious young tones; friendly lovers or loving friends, familiar with one another as with the Palatine. If not born Romans, they had acclimatized. They talked metaphysics, for whose discussion the lucid Italian language is so perfectly framed. "This beautiful house of sensation in which we live . . ." he said. (*"Questa bella casa di sensazione in quale viviamo . . ."*) The words made me their neighbour: I looked round, to see, stamped on the air, his profile intently turned, her full face abstract and calm with thought. Since, what has become of him? I must not forget him. Killed in the war against us? (Soon after that April, the war came.) If he still lives, I hope he still finds the house fair. *It* is still here. Is there so great a gap between the pure in sense and the pure in heart?

Matthew Arnold, son of the Dr. Arnold of my first evening, nevertheless speaks of "the howling senses." Possibly they do howl when they are outraged—they merit better. By the poet's reckoning, what zoolike echoings must have made these palaces subhuman! The Caesars housed themselves and their *entourages* not only in splendour but with a nonstop expansiveness which, soon eating up the limited hilltop, made for superimposition and overlapping. Excavation discloses floors beneath floors. Gorgeous extensions were grafted on to what predecessors, themselves not modest, had thought to be the palatial utmost. As we know, Augustus lived quietly in his wife's house: not the Palatine but the city and

Forum were to be made splendid by his monuments. Up here, Tiberius was the first to strike out: his palace continues to bear his name, though successively added to by Caligula, Domitian, Trajan, and Hadrian, till it ended by commanding the whole outlook over the (present) Via di San Teodoro. The dusky corridors underrunning the top plateau of the Farnese Gardens are part of the Palace of Tiberius: in the sunshine above them are box-edged flowerbeds, tree-planted gravel walks, friendly benches. The forehead (as it were) of the gardens is the dizzy-high terrace from which one beholds the Forum. The diminished Farnese Casino, mostly of glass, also has a Tiberian site; with, beneath it, a trickling rococo grotto in which the ferns are a just brighter green than the slime. The grotto invites you to pause, if you climb up that way.

(Alas, the Farnese Gardens themselves are no more than vestiges, today. Added to up to the eighteenth century, they once swept blandly downward into the Forum—or rather, stepped their way down in terraces. The Pannini drawing records an "effect" masterpiece: flight upon flight of steps florid as staircases, balustrades, façades, loggias, statues, urns, lawns. The late-Renaissance Farnese Cardinal outdid the Caesars at their own game, on their own ground. He saw no reason not to overbuild Antiquity, since he could better it. Posterity, however, failed to agree with him: the vertical part of the

gardens was shorn away in the interests of archae-
ology. Looking up at the seedy frontage exposed, I
often feel that the Cardinal knew best. And who
am I, that I should not have my say? You and I are
also posterity, after all.)

The aim of more than one Imperial builder was
to bridge the Palatine over to other hills. Caligula's
passage-way to the Capitol is now supposed to have
been of wood, for no trace remains: eventually, the
poor monster was trapped and murdered in a corridor of his own planning. Nero's Golden House and
its pleasure grounds were slung between the Palatine and the Esquiline: at the Palatine end it had
an underground system of connection with the Palace of Tiberius and Caligula, which in turn claimed
as part of itself the honeycomb through which a carriage road went down to the Forum. Unofficial descents into Rome, to satisfy lusts, were provided for
by a warren of ramps and staircases; for ceremonial
descents, in blazes of glory, arrangements were the-
atrically appropriate.

The third of the Flavian Emperors disentangled
himself, when he began to build, from the Julio-
Claudians. The Palace of Domitian filled in what
had been a declivity in the centre of the Palatine—
and what remains of a part of it should be sought
out: these roofless halls, their walls sere and jagged,
concentrate within themselves more illusion than do
any other ruins on the hill. The plan is clear; some-

how one feels surrounded by more than the eye sees. Columns are gone; the fountain-basins are dry; the niches are as empty of their statues as are the apses of the Emperor's person. You pass from the *triclinium,* in which he banqueted to aquatic music, to the throne-room which staged him, then into the basilica in which he administered justice as he saw it. The proportions, the interrupted rhythm of broken carvings combine to lure one through as it were a succession of burst bubbles. It is in the *triclinium* that heaved-up pavements, undulating like a sea of marble, invite you to step from colour to colour. This was what it was like to be an Emperor, in the overpowering presence of Oneself. And Domitian had another companion: fear. Certain, and rightly, of being sooner or later stolen up upon, he caused the walls of the *peristyle,* phengite marble, to be polished till they became mirrors—reflected, he watched what went on behind him. His nerves must have felt the assassin's blade hundreds of times before it struck.

What we have beheld, however, are state rooms only. The residential part of the Palace of Domitian extends elsewhere—its is the long, long frontage, porches and windows staring towards the Aventine, which overhung our scramble along the dog-path. The Emperor had a stadium in the building; unless this round-ended enclosure were a pleasure-garden. Down into halls and apartments, like empty bear-pits, one gazes from the ramparts, *pericoloso*. There is too much of them; they have an air of having been sulkily brought to daylight. Better the Villa Mills.

The Villa Mills was, like the Farnese Gardens, an optimistic latecomer to the Palatine—indeed, the last architectural flowering of the hope of pleasure. Sited atop a then-buried portion of the Domitian palace, it was originally the Villa Spada, sixteenth-century, with a portico joyously frescoed with gods and goddesses, and everything to be wished in the way of a view. Charles Mills, a bachelor Scot who arrived in Rome with a young man taken to be his adopted son, acquired the property in 1818: having restored the Renaissance portico, he went on to encase the villa in neo-Gothic. It was exquisite. Patriotic thistles adorned his gateposts, and reappeared, intertwined with emblematic roses and shamrocks, in medallions between many pointed arches. His garden was fragrant with jasmine, heliotrope, living roses. Though by some found "eccentric" and unrewarding, Mills in his bower of delights was beset by callers—otherwise, his existence was one many an Emperor might have envied. Some years after his death (1846: he lies in Rome's Protestant Cemetery) the villa became a convent of the Order of the Visitation. The nuns added a wing, which, shorn-off, remains: permitted to survive the rest of the structure, it now is the Palatine Museum (which I have never succeeded in finding open).

But the nuns, in time, took up their quarters elsewhere, leaving the villa to be immolated—demolition took place in 1926; the diggers, free to proceed
with work, went on to exhume the mournful Domitian halls. Few sympathize with the Palatine in its
loss of what guide-books stigmatize as "a sham."
But the Villa Mills was make-believe, in the tradition. Better, surely, a speaking fantasy than dumb
remnants? These latest parts of the palace to be exposed have as date, it is thought, 92 A.D.

Domitian enlarged the Palatine, at this side, by
the addition of masonry platforms on which he intended further to build. Of these, he had not time to
take advantage: Septimius Severus, however, used
them as foundations for his Baths. Gayer once than
now, the two floors of arches provided galleries from
which the Emperor's parties could watch the spectacles in the Circus Maximus, below. Also, Septimius
Severus did better—some way down from the Baths,
at the foot of the hill, where the Via Appia set off on
its southward journey, he brought into being the
Septizonium, a building distinguished by having no
other function than that of dazzling incoming travellers. This, from every account, it must have done—
façade for façade's sake, the thing consisted of seven
tiers of polished columns and flashing fountains.
Were the Septizonium not gone, it would face, today,
on the Via di San Gregorio—its remains were swept
away by Pope Sixtus V, who thought them foolish

and needed the marble. Nothing now deflects the eye of the motorist from the Arch of Constantine and the Colosseum.

The Palatine taught me what emptiness can be. Life has run out completely: one is alone there. Those existences, artificial as fireworks, have like fireworks died out on the forgetful dark. Of the Emperors, Nero seems to have lived longest, through having begotten a superstition—more than one are his fictitious "tombs"; a walnut tree had to be cut down because he infested it in the form of black, flapping birds. What was done to him, that he did this to Rome? I make off downhill, in the dusk, on the heels of the dog-walkers: night, floating with lights, is already into the city. Night is recurrent. The long day in which I continue to live has been sliced by nights. There is an alikeness between all and any nights in the same place; therefore the people in it, those who were, those who are, are probably most alike when they are asleep, and, still more, when they are not asleep but should be. People are most themselves when suddenly woken, or when they pull darkness over their heads, or when, in the middle of the night, they commit themselves to some momentous decision.

III

ON SUCH A NIGHT

MANY ROMANS under the Empire were bad sleepers; insomnia, I learn, was a fairly general condition. Various opiates were resorted to; sleep otherwise was for impervious children, the drunk, the physically exhausted, those pacified by dullness of mind or with a trend to oblivion in spite of everything.

In Rome I knew no horrible waking hours. I had an absolute sleep which I called Roman; I know no sleep like it anywhere else. Every night, it sought me rather than I it. If noon shutter-banging rattled and discomposed me, midnight's had the reverse effect.

This was no more than Rome going off the air. Cinemas disgorging their last audiences, bars throwing out clients, repartee shouted under my windows, Vespas being kicked till they roared alive came through from a disconnected universe; neon-reflections on walls or ceiling coloured the dreamy periphery of my dreamlessness. Granted, day after day I had been at large, on foot, in the open air, with no care but Rome. Obstinate was my sleep, till it found itself to require a breathing-space between three and four in the morning. By then, it was a luxury or holiday to be conscious. Not a footstep often was to be heard, near me or anywhere in the city; everything had been quenched but the street-lighting— lamps which, strung along the perspectives, brought into half-existence some yellow buildings against the black velvet curtain of Rome's extinction. The lamps themselves slumbered; to look out of a window was to look into sleep's many lidless eyes. Silence swallowed up distances: nearer dawn came notes from birds in the ilexes of the Pincio; later, Rome's country-town day could be heard beginning with the incoming rattle of market carts. There is a season of the year when sheep are by night driven through Rome, from their winter to summer pastures. This I missed, but a friend helped me picture it. Having lately moved into lodgings in the Corso, he was wakened in the small hours by a sound so unmistakable yet improbable that he lay puzzling, till he settled the matter by looking out. Flocks, whose backs from above were like small clouds curdling under a plane, streamed under his balcony, seldom bleating, with a soft-flanked jostling, sedate clicking of steps. What an image, how perfect a soporific, to summon on to the screen of a sleepless brain!—but he did not need them. They progressed down the fashionable carriage-way, at last to vanish; he returned to his pillow.

Rome for the ancient Romans was, however, unbearably modern. Imagine the twentieth century undergone by those not yet fitted for or inured to it! With regard to nights, there were regulations or absence of regulations which worked unhappily— one example, the law forbidding wheeled traffic in the city by day. This meant that everything, *everything,* was unpent at nightfall. Wagons and chariots surged through tortuous streets (which were sounding-boxes), colliding and interlocking, desperately racing against cockcrow. The struggle to be extricated from Rome, head-on against those who were forging into it, took place—when there was not a moon—in darkness: there was no street-lighting. The streets, where intermissions in traffic made this possible, were accordingly given over to crime and lust. Respectable citizens bolted themselves in and retired early; through the chinks in their shutters there now and then entered a whirling ruddiness— torches convoying nefarious pleasure-parties. And more threatening glares, also, disturbed the worthy: houses were constantly bursting into flames. A dropped lamp or kicked-over brazier could be enough; dwellings were easy tinder. Apart from Rome's major, historic fires, outbreaks took unreckoned toll of life and property. So far as I know, nobody was insured. And yet another reason to lie worrying was that buildings were liable to fall down. Run up on the cheap by contractors to reckless heights of four or it might be five storeys, the *insulae* (or tenement houses) were unsteady: thunderous glissading collapses, extinguished shrieks might, any night, rend the ears of neighbours.

More than one of the Emperors took note, whether advisedly or kind-heartedly, of these bad conditions. Augustus, when ordaining the survey of the city, the division into regions, the drawing-up of the definitive huge map, had foreseen trouble with skyscrapers: his was the edict which forbade erection of buildings over three storeys—it was got round, by lovers of dizzy height, by raising the nominal bases on piles or pillars. The otherwise infamous Caligula was among later would-be reformers. Attempts were from time to time made to police the streets; a fire-guard service was inaugurated. It was, however, impossible for those officially charged with public safety to be everywhere at once. Nothing could be done about the traffic, and anti-vice squads would not have been in the interest of the Palatine.

97

In the main, such measures as were introduced did little to uproot fatalistic fear—the worst *might* not happen, nevertheless one expected that it would. Apprehension reigned, for most Romans going to bed. You and I, who complain about insecurity, have yet to envisage it as a concrete circumstance— in a city at peace, world-dominant, gorged with wealth.

There is a surviving example of an *insula* (expertly disencrusted from later buildings) backed into the Capitoline hill, on the Piazza di Venezia side. Those interested in housing should stop and look at it. Ample as to windows, solid in structure, it accommodated middle-class families, who by our standards could have fared worse. In its favour, also, is that it is still standing. Clearly, though, this is one of the better type; from which the *insulae* graded down to gimcrack warrens, rank, slummy, swarming. (More remains of "the best" can be seen at Ostia Antica; where, according to reconstruction, they sported awnings and flowery balconies, providing apartments for *rentiers* who today in England would dwell at Folkestone, Bournemouth, or Eastbourne). Rome's more respectable *insulae* flanked on the quite pestiferous. All had the characteristic of being undrained, unheated. Ovens in summer, they were in winter perforated by icy draughts. Little or none was furniture; for one thing, it cost too much, for another, owing to humans there was not room for it. The interior dreariness of the *insulae* to an extent was due to, to an extent begat, domestic apathy on the part of the tenants, who conceived of life (in any livable sense) as a thing to be lived in public, outdoors on the streets, *en masse,* in an atmosphere of festivity where possible or anger when occasion demanded. Much of Rome was populated by born crowds—in which particular it has not greatly altered. One turns home, in this capital, reluctantly, when anything more enticing has ceased to offer. As to sleep, the *insulae* dwellers, crisscrossed like rushes three-deep on floors, probably did better than their betters on Roman beds. They had less to think about.

Roman beds of the time of the Empire, as shown to us, seem framed to promote nervous rigidity. They are to be lain on rather than in. Narrow, racklike, with sharply turned-up heads, they would appear to be the enemies of voluptuousness, no less than of relaxation. Amorous excess, of which we hear so much, took place on these inhospitable couches—may vices and variations not have been the by-products of discomfort? Did having been begotten on such beds account for that anxious bleakness of temperament manifest in many outstanding Romans? I remind myself that masters of these beds reclined so much and so stylishly in the daytime that they may have desired no change at night. A male patrician, when not standing or walking, was horizontal: extended he dined, he received company—which, if he were a person of wealth and consequence, to a degree consisted of hangers-on. The hanger-on system, it would appear, was built into gilded Roman society: a considerable number of persons of lesser means, though sufficient claims to gentility, busied themselves in making themselves agreeable, building their patron's morale up by adulation, while simultaneously subtly undermining it by disturbing rumours, hints, disclamatory titters, and protestations of loyalty come what might. Such conversation left behind food for thought, particularly at three o'clock in the morning. The ignominious pattern provides fun, in any caricature of success society: look for it in Restoration comedy, or the French, or any satirical theatre worth attending—simply, in Rome the margin between ridicule and catastrophe was narrower. Bad as it feels to look silly, it is worse to be dead. The Empire was a regime under which it was always to someone's interest that someone else should fall—what began as gossip could culminate in ruin or the executioner's strangling-noose, or both (with the possible "out" of suicide). No wonder the man of clear conscience was not only extolled but envied—no other dared throw a satellite out. The toadies were always accomplices, often spies, and everyone knew it—the cost of such gratification as they afforded was to know oneself in their power, and in deep. There was no knowing to whom they might not take themselves off, next. The statuesque pose of recline adopted by leading Romans (as though anticipating adorning tombs) did, however, place them at one advantage: they could *appear* languid and imperturbable. Masters of households, they had the air of being masters of the situation—as they were, till it came to their night thoughts.

How far dyspepsia contributed to the wakefulness is an open question. The lengthiness and richness of Roman banquets has been emphasized to the point of boredom. Also harped upon is the fact that guests disembarrassed their stomachs, halfway through, by induced vomiting. This device, for which provision was made, I can see no reason to criticize: it was far from general—many people found no need to resort to it, having dined in their own or their friends' homes deliciously, sparingly, and simply, in small numbers, fanned by cooling air, with the sound of a fountain as background to memorable conversation. These were the great; encompassed, it is true, by their own dangers, but outside contamination, so not pitiable. Also not present at banquets, apart from those not invited, were those who preferred to keep out of trouble—parties of remarkable ostentation are apt to be given for some reason, it may well be a fishy one. There was what would now be called "the Palatine set," but the pleasures of that distinction were dubious—the Emperors were given to ghastly tricks, such as dressing the servitors as skeletons. Or one might be present when one's Imperial host was dragged, convulsed by death-agonies, from the revels—in that case, on whom might not suspicion fall? Or an enemy might have denounced one, just before dinner; or the Emperor might denounce one, all on his own. The Emperors liked the rich, but liked riches better: conveniently, the wealth of those convicted of treason passed direct into the Imperial coffers. Many were the uncertainties, whose effect on the gastric juices cannot have been propitious.

Tranquil or otherwise the occasion, I still think the attitude of the diner cannot have made for correct digestion. One reclined along-and-across couches; each couch, as a rule, held three diagonal diners at a time. One ate with the right-hand fingers, the bowl or platter being held in the left; and throughout one had to support oneself on one's left elbow. To get at drink, one had to stretch some way for the goblet, which between times occupied a low table. There was added the business of constant hand-washing, necessary but disturbing, in bowls of scented water brought to the couches. As I see it, the twistedness of the torso during eating must have correspondingly twisted the stomach-muscles, further strained by reachings-out for the wine. "Sit up straight and give your stomach a chance!" was advice boomed at Edwardian children at schoolroom meals, and a lifetime has taught me it was sound. Romans' dining posture surely impeded Nature. Yet, even suppose them to have been the worse for this, were they not the better for two things, devotion to ceremonial, faith in tradition? Once one breaks with either, endless unease begins.

To what, at the end of an evening, did one return? Though wealthy homes spread outward over the hills, the Esquiline, Caelian, and Aventine, the conservative remained wedged in the heart of Rome. There appears to have been no watertight social zoning; city-dwellers of all ranks lived cheek-by-jowl. M. Jerome Carpocino sees the amalgam darkly—"Imperial Rome," he says, "was continually forced to juxtapose her splendid monuments to an incoherent confusion of dwelling houses at once pretentious and uncomfortable, fragile and inordinately large, separated by a network of gloomy alleys." Today the Campus Martius, jumble of slums and palaces, remains nearest to the ancient conditions. Segregation according to means or class, unhappily begun in the nineteenth century, does away with much of the birthright of being Roman. . . . As things were, the late home-goer, body-guarded, would plunge through a fair cross-section of nocturnal chaos. Once he had crossed his threshold, the worst was over—night's most gruelling torment was left behind; traffic sounded faintly, at last excluded.

For, whereas the many-tenanted *insula* opened directly upon the street, the *domus* (private house, in the hands of one family) was arranged otherwise. The *domus* turned to the street an unbroken wall, blind of apertures but for the entrance doorway. (Such walls, I saw in Pompeii: they make the long-empty thoroughfares still blanker.) Inside was a courtyard, which, when full-grown, the dwelling surrounded on three sides. In plan, and pattern of life, the *domus* centred upon the *atrium:* this, of imposing proportions, served sacred, domestic, and social time-honoured purposes—compared to the rest of the house it was semi-public: only the privileged visitor passed beyond it. Occupying ample, expensive ground-space, the *domus* could scorn ostentatious height: seldom was it of more than two storeys, though here or there might be elevated a terrace roof. Palisaded against the outside world, those within the *domus* do not seem to have sought any great degree of privacy from each other—often, no more than curtains over the doorway divided the enfiladed rooms, of which many had painted walls.

Wall-paintings, from a Roman *domus* lately exhumed, have been transferred to an upstairs gallery of the Museo Nazionale, near the railway station. They should be enjoyed on a sleepy wet afternoon. They give off an atmosphere, being at once luminous and shadowy—and they have surprising freshness: partially here or there a design may have perished or been splintered, but mainly wax has so ingrained the colours into the plaster that Pompeian red, watery ink-black, turquoise, gold-ochre, silvery olive-green, bluish or tawny pinks, and nacreous flesh-tints look as though not having faded they now could not. Swags of fruit or flowers, pastoral scenes, *amorini,* lyricized moments of home or fashionable life or religious observance are among the ever-pleasing, unoriginal subjects. Faintly Chinese influence shows in bamboos, pavilions. Fondness for animals, link with us Anglo-Saxons, is bespoken; as again, repeatedly, in the mosaic floor pavements and fountain-bottoms. Though elsewhere, in the Museo del Laterano, we see a domestic floor-pattern of brutish pugilists—or did these come from baths, or a club?—the general trend of the decorations is to the feminine: woman's taste or what that is taken to be. Nothing about these paintings, minute and sensuous, releases one into the air of art: if anything, their effect might be claustrophobic. The aim was not to enlarge existence but to flatter it. And day-to-day existence, one may imagine, *was* confirmed in the character it already had by these idealizing and soothing representations which hemmed it in.

But if the paintings were static, the rooms were not—on the contrary, they must be envisaged as stages crossed by frequent and all but unending processions. Slaves were if anything more numerous than their many functions. Space, in the *domus,* was not encumbered by anything not necessary at the moment: what was required for an elaborate toilet, or if not that for a repast or refreshment, or if not that for secretarial activity, study, recreation, or display was accordingly constantly being borne in or out. Immovable furniture was limited—mobile containers for clothing, cosmetics, papers, valuables, and so on were provided by chests, coffers, and caskets. Rooms, for the greater part of the day, were subject to scene-shifting, transformation. There came, however, the hour when looped-up curtains were lowered, and all was stilled. Last lamps, left burning in the silence, multiplied the shadows awaiting the master of the house. Last slaves yawned at their posts, till his step was heard.

Weighed upon by his all but sacerdotal role, he returned to become the centre of pressing forces. A minute back, I spoke of the *domus* as being the private house of a single family—that, inadequate, could lead to a misconception. An infinity of wider meanings attached to it. For us, "the sanctity of the home" is a wishful myth; the sanctity of the *domus* was indisputable. Most sacred, to Romans, of institutions, it was not less so for having been instituted by them. Nothing equivalent had been given birth to by any of the foregoing civilizations. The Greeks had had nothing of the kind: the *domus,* therefore, provided one firm base for Rome's sense of moral superiority. As for us, in so far and for so long as home is a concept, rather than a container for things and persons, we continue to be in debt to the Romans. With us, lately, the concept has watered itself down, becoming more sentimental, less legalistic. (Or at least, that is so with us Anglo-Saxons; Latin races, whose home life seems to us rigid, probably keep closer to the original.) The *domus* enshrined tradition, subordinated egotism, and bred virtues which extended their value outside its walls. It was the private source of the public character, educated, temperate, disciplined. While there was nothing new about the conception of an ideal society the conception of an ideal unit, to be a domestic one, had been a step forward. The Republican high idea of the *domus*, which had been justified, lived on under the Empire, for a long time after rot had begun to attack the actual structure. It survived if largely as a reproach.

The *domus* was an example of authority, absolute, vested in the master, *paterfamilias*. His authority, which law defined and supported, was enhanced by having a mystic aspect. Something above humanity was asked of the designated man—just as his household (family, dependents, servitors) were welded into more than a household, he himself was more than householder, husband, father. Yet this was not, as with the successors of Augustus, a case of a role impossible to fill; it had been so filled as to create a prototype. Tradition expected of the *paterfamilias* three attributes: gravity, simplicity, piety. (The Latin nouns are more spacious in connotation than our English ones, which give but a shrunken view of the Roman outlook.) Absence of passion, veneration for justice, would, it was taken, characterize his dealings with the children he had engendered, the slaves he owned, the blood-relations he elected to shelter. Nor were his dealings with humans only. A census taken of the *domus, per capita,* would render no true account of its inhabitants, of whom a considerable further number were supernatural. There were powers with whom the *paterfamilias* was forever in treaty. A *domus* was the protectorate of special divinities—in the hearth dwelled Vesta, spirit of the flame, in the store-cupboard the Penates, spirits of provision. (I speak of a city *domus:* one in the country would, also, feel the pervasive presence of the Lars, favourable to land.) Gladly were tributes rendered to such guardians. But less friendly forces could be at work; deities, ever capricious, could turn hostile—there was necessarily the anxious business of buying off ill-will, averting, if possible, misfortune. There could be infestations; hosts of elementals, ragtag and bobtail, were apt to release themselves into the Roman home. Propitiatory offerings to deities, preventive measures against nuisances, kept the altars smoking, the master busy. Upon *paterfamilias* devolved the performance of many rites. How effective were they?

One was not to know. One fascination, for me, of the Roman temperament at the time I speak of, is its blend of constructive will with supine fatalism. Apprehensions riddled those men of purpose. Virtue ensured nothing—which made it, surely, as an aim grander, as an achievement purer? The Gods neither inspired nor comforted—how could they? As I see them, which is not how Rome saw them, they presented images of power-mania plus instability—who were they to jib at consorting with the Emperors who from time to time elected to join their ranks? Taken over from the Greeks, the Gods seem never to have been subjected to close scrutiny: to instate them, having re-named them, appeared enough. To worship was necessary. Since their Hellenic morning, the Gods seem steadily to have lost height. Dazzlingness, primitiveness, and poetry departed from them. Did they (to do them justice) feel themselves *dépaysés, déclassés,* at once misfitted and irked by their Roman moulds? For whatever reason, here they were at their worst. Vast as could be their anger, its causes were depressingly trivial; when they struck out, it was to avenge some misunderstood wish or unfed vanity. Blindly were they honoured; disproportionate were the thanks that went to them for what could be taken to be benevolence. I cannot think of the Gods without indignation on behalf of the good Romans with whom they played cat-and-mouse. Yet the protractedness, bloodiness, bitterness, and complexity of the struggle necessary to unseat them show how much they had come to mean. A bad buy, they evoked much that was noble in Roman obstinacy. (Firm stood those who adhered to them as a losing cause; honour should go to the pagan martyrs.) Rome's being a state religion made it not merely obligatory or an affair of lip-service: the Gods had been underwritten by the State, and we know what fervour, devotion, altruism, and piety the State commanded, how exalting the idea of it was to a good mind, how sublime could be dedication to its service. Yet deities made marble by public function can in no way have touched the realities of the soul, guided its anxious course or assuaged its longings. I have the impression that personal Roman religion was unofficial. Animism, the attribution of spiritual being to natural objects, played some part in it, plus an inadvertent and for the most part anonymous mysticism. Seek, and ye shall find. Were there not veritable Beings who were indigenous, as the Gods were not?—earth and water spirits, bidders of springs, blessers of groves, together with geniuses of places? Existence felt a strong non-rational undertow, though whether to the dark or the light it could not be said. And from the pre-inhabited ground itself came effluences one could not counter; the Romans were late-comers in a land saturated by religions, no one of which had entirely spent its force. One cannot believe that races subordinated, extirpated, or driven out had left nothing behind them, or that mysterious vestiges of altars were not for ever stimulating the hunger they partly fed. There had been a primitive harmony when Rome first rose; under the Empire there was a widening rift between inner need and outer observance. Cults from the East multiplied—sterling persons denounced them, fought shy of them, misliked them. The excellent wish of the Roman was to be adult; this in general he realized in his deportment, his social discipline, his regard for law. His unaccounted-for soul was, by contrast, childish. In an orbit of her own reigned the Magner Mater, misty with largeness, and primordial. How far was she to be turned to by the man in the dark?

Just as fear of the building falling accounted for some of the wakefulness in an *insula,* the master of a *domus,* in the small hours, had to fight against a dread of collapse—in this case, not of the house but its good name. Nothing could be more final than dishonour: political treachery or financial scandal were but two of the ways by which it could come about. Example had been set by that Roman father who slew his son for bringing disgrace upon their house—the sad act had occasioned a *cause célèbre: had* the *paterfamilias* the right to put into practice his theoretic power of life-and-death? The implacable Roman notion of honour finds nearest modern equivalent in Spain, and its counterpart, I under-

stand, in Japan. The code had been rigid; it still
was so for those who abided by it under the Empire.
Rome now was thronged, however, by a new up-
start class who made light of the code, made fun of
it or had never heard of it, and intolerably throve on
its contravention. Freedmen, who had got themselves out of slavery by intelligence, then gone on to
carve out careers and amass fortunes, were in particular loathed by the *ancien régime*. Orientals,
Jews, ambiguous Greeks, flourishing as profiteers
or racketeers, were taking over the town: they too
were anathema. Their flashy homes in the newer
suburbs contradicted every idea of living stood for
by the superciliously modest *domus*. They gave
spectacular feasts, to which many went—the *paterfamilias* wondered, for how much longer were his
own young people to be restrained from going? Bad
wealth was making hay of the class system—always
more easily rotted than abolished. . . . Corruption,
temptations from the most insidious to the most
blatant, were everywhere, on all sides, outside the
domus. Almost everybody was deviating from something, whether in the ethical, sexual, or religious
field. Greek intelligentsia, like deathwatch beetles,
were at work in the Roman intellectual structure.
Seeing in his mind's eye, as he lay in the dark, the
faces of his still blameless children, the *paterfamilias*
must have asked himself which would be the one to
grow up to sell the fort, and in what manner, and

how soon? Or would it be himself—through some some inadvertence, blind spot, or moral miscalculation? (Aged Marshal Pétain, I remember, at his trial expounded what had been his lifelong principle: when the path of duty appears to divide, or fork, take whichever path of the two is for you the harder. The sheer costliness, to oneself, of a line of conduct may bedevil one into taking it for the right one.) A man might be implicated in evil before he knew. . . . Again, nothing of the sort might happen: it might, but might not. So much depended. Round went the brain's millwheel—self-scrutiny, backward analysis of doings, morbid examination of so-called friends for symptoms of what might be infectious venality. Then, at last, for a short and austere space, sleep. The *paterfamilias* rose early, thereby at once (one may hope) shaking off the night and setting an example to his household, who followed it—the hour at which otherwise leisurely Romans began the day surprises me; however, it has been vouched for. A long ceremonial toilet prepared him to face the world and countenance visitors: as soon as might be, he took himself off to the Forum. The *domus*, for the greater part of the day, remained under the management of women, whose position under the Roman marriage laws was good.

Roman dreads were not fantasies. Magnified as they might be by the small hours, they were neither needless nor feverish apprehensions; each one repre-

sented a possibility. Akin to the danger to honour
was the more concrete danger of dispossession—
seizure of home and property. Machinations against
one, actual culpability or the bringing of a charge
one failed to disprove could bring this about: to
material loss, for those driven out, could not fail to
be added the dissolution of the *domus* as a spiritual
estate. The dwelling itself was either demolished,
vindictively, or passed into other, profaning hands.
"Is there anything," Cicero demanded, "more hal-
lowed, is there anything more closely hedged around
by sanctity than the home of each individual citizen?
Therein he has his altars, his private worships, his
rites and ceremonies. For all of us this is a sanctuary
so holy that to tear a man away from it is an outrage
to the law of heaven." The orator spoke in his own
cause, of his own case, and from the heart. Cicero,
back again, was pleading for the restoration of his
home, destroyed by enemies when he was forced
into exile the year before. This was 56 B.C.: he commanded an audience which, if proofed against sentiment, could be appalled by sacrilege. He addressed
himself to Romans of his own kind—how far Cicero's "all of us" extended beyond such hearers, I do
not know. That is, how far did the law of heaven
operate for a patch of floor-space, contended for by
families, in an *insula?* The canonization of the
domus, as an idea, took place at a fortunate level:
how far can sanctity travel downward? Leave it that

to be dispossessed is horrible. To the banished races this was already known.

I note the Roman attitude to calamity. Cicero, in invoking the law of heaven, invoked what was by nature *of* heaven: law—inviolable principle, better than the vacillating Gods. This was the sacrosanct— "it is written." Ready to bow to calamity as a stroke of fate, Romans resisted it as an outrage. Very much depended upon the light in which a calamity was to be seen, or shown.

Sleep was to be dreaded by whichever one of the six Vestal Virgins was on night duty in the circular temple. Round her, as she watched Vesta's fire's sacred reflections pulse on the inside of the white dome, would sound stray unaccountable footsteps about the Forum, its acoustics sharpened by night. The ear of the girl or woman (ages of Vestals being from fifteen upward to forty-five) would attune itself, at once intently and blankly, as though to the syllables of a foreign language, to the give-offs of a world of which she knew little—some lonely, nervous, aggressively planted tread, alcoholic zigzagging, the sound-track of one person creeping upon another across pavement, ratlike slippings and scurryings of those still furtive though now hidden. Couplings, accompanied by sounds corresponding to nothing in her experience—human, it was to be supposed—would be taking place under nearby porticoes; and now and then a leap of preyer on prey, a dulled fall like that of a sack of earth, pettish dying-down flailing of limbs, death-gurgles. Herself, she had nothing but sleep to fear. The element she nursed, as it beat upward, tinged her face with the only flame it would know. If she fell asleep and let the fire out, a priest would beat her; he would perform this office chastely, correctly, in the modest dark. The penalty, bereft of interest by punctilio, would be less awful than the dead-black extinction on which she *might* open her eyes, if for so much as a moment she dared risk closing them. I have wondered whether, ironically, a Vestal forcing herself awake through the small hours, swimmy in the warmth, hypnotized by the flame's flutter, was not often the one genuine sleepyhead in polite Rome. As against that, nerves might be kept on the stretch: young nurses speak of the arid abnormality of a night watch—not the duty (which is a mitigation) but the watch itself tells terribly on the spirit and strains the consciousness. Something about it, they say, is against Nature. Hours in which the dying easily die are those least livable for the living. The Vestal, peculiarized since childhood, may not have reacted to her ordeal thus. Night and day, now I come to think of it, must have been much the same in that small closed temple, whose beehive hut form commemorated the early days of the cult. Yet I cannot think one can defy night and not be aware of it.

The five other Vestals were free to slumber, in

their row of bedchambers in the Atrium, and everything suggests that they should have done so, soundly. Their day had been tranquil, ordered, piously pleasant. Their surroundings, as we know, were delightful; moreover the spacious plan of the precincts gave them no reason to get on each other's nerves—they had no need to mix when not in the mood. They had no economic anxieties, and no emotional ones if they had sense. Unlike nuns (with whom they are not to be confused) the Vestals led a by no means cloistered existence; hardly a day went by without an outing. In daylight they could whirl round Rome in carriages, that privilege denied to everyone else; and they appeared, seated near the Emperor, at all public ceremonials, spectacles, and functions. The circus, the race course, and later the Colosseum were nothing when not graced by their presence: they inhaled sweat and crowd stenches as they might the scent of flowers in their *peristyle* garden, were unruffled by passions and pandemonium, gazed unblinkingly down into troughs of bloodshed. Their dress, a tunic over a pleated robe, the head being bound by a fillet, was becoming. (The fillet, in the form of a *rouleau,* rose high above the unfurrowed brow—in some portrait statues this may give the impression, a wrong one, that they wore their hair *en Pompadour.*) Each Vestal, offspring of an aristocratic *domus,* had undergone searching examination before being accepted for the Order: not only morality and intelligence were required of her, she had also to be found physically perfect—not only without defect or disability but, one may take it, at least reasonably good-looking. Having been accepted, she had to wait; for the candidate was brought for examination at the age of not more than five or six. The girl child was brought to the Atrium, one imagines, less by her own choice (except in cases of great precocity) than at the instance of her determined family. For a daughter, no higher honour was to be sought; and the young set-apart creature, waiting at home for her fifteenth birthday and/or the next vacancy in the Atrium, probably learned to regard herself, as did those round her, with sacred enthusiasm. If there were recalcitrants, I have not heard of them.

The existences of the Vestal Virgins were, as I see it, enviable. For what they forwent as women, they were compensated in the ways women most truly enjoy. An aura surrounded them. Limelit appearances, during which everything that they said and did was above criticism, alternated with restful privacy. Their transit through streets or across the Forum left behind it a wake of awe, not untouched by sentiment, in the most profane. They were on idyllic terms with Emperors with whom it would otherwise have been impossible to be platonic. So far as the great could relish intelligence, the six had an opportunity to show it. The elevated seclusion in which they lived must have been favourable to the growth of character, as is conditioned air to the nurseling plant. Vestals' counsels were harkened to; they could exercise influence, and did so. They could secure pardons: a Vestal meeting in the street a criminal being taken to execution could have him spared. Sheathed from grossnesses, insulated from dramas, scandals, the six during their sallies into the *beau monde* were free to observe these at close quarters: much must they have had to discuss, with a cool wonder, upon their return to the cool Atrium. Yet they knew, one may hope, something more than serene complacency; rendered to religion by dedication, they cannot but have been spiritualized by their unearthly duties. Moreover, what they saw of the flesh must have beautified for them their vow of chastity.

Chastity was very strictly enforced; a Vestal who lapsed was buried alive—she descended into a subterranean tomb which was then sealed up over her head. If punctilio attended upon a beating, still more was it present at the infliction of death: the cell-like tomb was furnished with food and drink, for a sacred lady must not die of starvation, and with gruesome respectfulness did the executioner assist the doomed one on to and down the ladder which took her to her protracted agony. However, given the long roll of the Vestal Virgins, lapses were rare. At forty-five a Vestal, released from the Order, was free to marry: should she elect to do so, what better wife for a distinguished, sober, correctness-esteeming widower? But there were those who preferred not to quit the Atrium. The position of Senior Vestal, probably reached, would make anything in the outside world seem an anti-climax. Those who chose not to abdicate could stay on, thereby blocking promotion and leaving some junior, next on the list for admission, to chafe at home well on into her teens—or even her twenties—for the number of Vestals might not exceed six.

The premises known as the Atrium of the Vestal Virgins were, we recall, more than once rebuilt, lavishly, by well-meaning Emperors. Each time this must have raised dust, disorganized routine, and brought in workmen. A more trying because more regular nuisance would have been night-time disturbance by the Palatine set—the Vestals must have been constantly shocked awake. The Atrium, remember, backed on the Palatine, which rose steeply above it like a wall, and the Vestals, again remember, slept at the back. Soon after the Forum's roar had subsided, activity would begin on the built-up hillside. That now spectral honeycomb, stairs, ramps, passages, through which moreover zigzagged a vaulted roadway, overhung the Atrium's bedchambers—and it was by one or another of those routes that after-dinner Palatine parties, on noisy vice bent, plunged their way down into the sink of unlit Rome, and ultimately made their debauched return. The din, the echoes they kicked up must have been hideous. The Imperial ladies and their *entourages* went to all lengths to flaunt their errors: consequently their names have remained so bad that there seems no point in blackening them further. Among the disappointments of Augustus had been Julia, his daughter and only child, whose desire for notoriety (possibly in opposition to her father) was realized. Widely broadcast, dangerously scandalous, her career had to be put a stop to: she was banished to an island, leaving behind her a train of smirched reputations and ruined lovers. Her daughter the second Julia was little better: between them the two set a pace which their successors felt nothing if they did not follow. Where would our vocabulary be without Messalina? Yet was not this Empress, now a prototype, but an extreme example of her kind?—who, adding to nymphomania an addiction to dabbling in power politics, in almost all cases met wretched ends. What mattered was, that they cost more than they were worth: they damaged the existing regard for women. The Roman matron—wise and temperate consort, guardian of everything in the *domus* that was benevolent and tender, raiser of memorable sons—came to be a receding and dimming image. Nor, for a time, did anything more individualized, original, or spirited replace her. The one career open to women outside the *domus* appeared to be a career round town; every caterwaul or titter heard in the night went to confirm masculine pessimism. Rome seems to have raised no "new woman" till the emergence of the feminine Christian martyrs, whose independence of character, equanimity, poise, firmness, and power to discountenance should be noted, not as distinct from their saintliness but as part of it. These were the emancipates, under God. Faith, and the necessity to testify, stirred awake in them qualities owed to an old heredity, a tradition which had at least nursed them, if it had also caused them, till now, to slumber.

Night, that of an ignorance not mine only, inundates my idea of the Dark Ages—the pause which followed the fall of Rome. I think of the dense, heavy night of some late autumn, which not only veils the scene but absorbs it into its morbid hush. Actually, Rome "fell"—when? Not built in a day, Rome did not fall in one—arguably it never fell at all; rather, decline steepened into a series of precipice-drops. Decline attracts catastrophes, of which each one serves to further decline. Rome was besieged, entered, and sacked by barbarians four times: in A.D. 410 by Alaric the Goth; in 455 by Genseric the Vandal; in 537 by Vitiges the Goth; in 546 by Totila the Ostrogoth. I understand that the first invaders were caused by awe of Rome to restrain their fury; those later found less there to inhibit them. All four of the outrages were suffered by a Rome already outraged by being gelded—so far back as A.D. 330, the Emperor Constantine had removed the central government to his new city on the Bosporus, Constantinople. How far his foreseeingness, or realism, as to the barbarian threat to the Western Empire coincided with Imperial vanity, I do not know. The admitted collapse of the Western Empire, in A.D. 476, justified his decision. From then on Rome, twice already entered and sacked, and due to be entered and sacked twice more, was ruled by a viceroy from Constantinople: evidently his presence was not heartening.

Those left in sunken Rome had little to say. It seems likely that so many disasters stripped them of ability to be sad consciously. More positive characters had gone—aristocrats and artisans, some time ago, into the promising sunrise of the Bosporus, property-owners in flight before the despoilers. The barbarians themselves had not cared to stay: healthy Goths, Vandals, Goths, and Ostrogoths had surged through, swooping on anything left by their predecessors, then out again, before the place had time to give them the creeps. Many of the stayers-on would have been hybrids—discarded slaves, run-down descendants of the careerists from every part of the Empire who had, once, bought their way in, and a number of those queer fish, misfits, without ambition or origin, who swim best in puddles when the tide has gone out. This residuum would have become Roman chiefly by its association with the stones, its improvisations of shelter in ruins shared with owls and bats, its aimless poking about in rubble. In so far as they were Romans, they would have been the first, I imagine, for centuries, to be untroubled by sense of loss, not preyed on by nostalgic idealism. They were down to bedrock; their woes were concrete. Occasionally, with the effect of an old dog howling, a senile voice may have raised itself in lament—lament for who knew what, and who cared, now? Toppled-over statues stayed face down in the mud, nobody troubling to roll them over and read their faces, which, all stamped by the look of something not now to be comprehended, would probably have seemed very much the same.

The ineffective Aurelian Wall now enclosed wastelands, which had as their smoky nucleus the village Rome had become. Some of the ground, reclaimed, was given over to the growing of wheat; ploughs lurched over more than one of what had been Augustus's numbered city regions. Organization, necessary if they were to live, welded these vestiges of the Romans into a community, and there was more than that to it: they were Christian. This therefore was not all; there was immortality. The Pope, bishop of Rome, shepherd of his sheep, guarded the thinning flock among the wastelands. A light burned; consciousness could not wholly atrophy. Fear could still be caused—for instance, wolves got in and ran the streets after dark. Besiegers cut the Campagna aqueducts; supply ceased in the hilly parts of the city; people crowded down to live by the Tiber's edge, among what had been the temples and theatres of the Campus Martius. Here, virtually, ancient Rome breathed its last, and mediaeval Rome, a provincial city, was to come to birth.

To dwell on the Dark Ages would be unbearable, had they been the end. They were not, being no more than an interim between the Rome of the Caesars and the Rome of the Popes. On the Middle Ages, I cannot find it tempting to dwell at all. One could feel that they were endured by mankind in order that they might fascinate the historian—much emerged from them, but surely it requires an expert eye to see what, or how? Otherwise they appear an abhorrent whirlpool, so far lacking the direction and shape which for me are the attributes of history that they are more like a long, bad, over-packed, over-written historical novel. In Rome they seem out of the picture. They had to take place; nothing can wipe them out; but of what went on during those (roughly) thousand years, in Rome or for that matter anywhere else, I cannot imagine it possible to keep track. I looked up a few dates, and have held to those. The genius of Pope Gregory the Great (A.D. 590–604) helped Rome to recover from the Gothic wars; having rallied, Rome, together with the

Church, more and more resented being dictated to by Constantinople, seat of the Byzantine (or Eastern) Empire. The West felt itself increasingly put upon. To right the balance, Pope Leo III turned to Charlemagne, the vigorous Frankish king, whom he crowned Holy Roman Emperor in Rome, on Christmas Day of the year 800. The creation of the Holy Roman Empire did not act happily on Europe, which was from 800 onward racked and divided, owing to the failure of successive Popes and Emperors to see eye to eye, and that of powerful monarchs to keep out of the invariably ensuing conflicts: each hurled his weight on to one or the other side. Hampered by the prevailing confusion, mediaeval Rome got to its feet slowly. Attacks and sackings reached their climax in A.D. 1084, when fire-raising Normans from Sicily were called in by one of two rival Popes to expel the Emperor. Prior to that, there had been a longlasting, nightmarish threat from Islam: in the ninth century Saracens rushed in and burned St. Peter's. A lull, with regard to external enemies, set in after the Normans had shot their bolt, but this was not accompanied by internal peace—now was the moment for Rome's noblemen to give rein to a furious distaste for one another: they made over what remained of the ancient ruins into fortresses, from which they egged on their supporters. The miserable people fought in the streets like dogs. Chaos passed all bounds during the years

(1305–1373) of the "Babylonian Captivity"—i.e., when the Popes were constrained to remain in Avignon. In the twelfth century Rome made welcome her first tourists—the pilgrims who began to converge on the Holy City were not too pious to be sight-seers also. Largely, it was for their benefit that Rome's first guide-book, the *Mirabilia Romae,* was written, around 1150. Official Christian respect was for the first time accorded to pagan marvels. One which could not be recalled was the Pax Romana.

For the greater part, mediaeval Rome is no longer to be found on the Campus Martius, in which most of the ground is occupied, now, by what came before or after, a range from embedded colonnades to tramlines. Dominants are the Pantheon and the Piazza Navona, which blend their not irreconcilable beauties into the atmosphere. Middle-Agedness does, however, survive in pockets and lurk round corners in many parts of this low-lying tract which was once its own—without warning you find yourself engorged, for minutes which feel like an eternity, by alley-narrow, suspicious, dolorous streets, which deliver you only to one another, acting upon you like bad thoughts. These strange old streets, say enthusiasts for them, are full of the past—what do they mean, *the* past?—These strange old streets are saturated with blood; as much was shed here as in any arena. Encompassed by marshes, they were malarial; they were death-traps in times of plague.

Of the dwellings darkling at each other across them, only a few do actually, I suppose, date back so far as the Middle Ages, but all have got themselves tenanted by that adverse spirit. This is *very old,* as apart from ancient, Rome. It is rich, it is my duty to point out, in cramped dramas and semi-mystical anecdotes—in which Augustus Hare, when we accompanied each other on a walk, did his best to interest me. But, spokesman as he is, and beguiling showman, he failed to make me stop where he often wanted to. I kept clear or got quickly out of very old Rome, unless I was lost.

For relief, go to the Via Giulia—straight-ruled margin of the Campus Martius on the Tiber side. It begins behind the enormous Farnese Palace, which you cannot miss, and has the distinction of being spanned by an arch at the palace end. Half a mile long, it has a preternaturally calm look, as though it were its own picture in a book of engravings. Nagel's guide-book calls it the most beautiful sixteenth-century road in Rome; myself I think of it as a street —it is flanked, from beginning to end, by Renaissance buildings. The homogeneity of the Via Giulia is due to its having been brought into being by one man, Pope Julius II (1503–1513). Architecturally, it coruscates with Renaissance names—Bramante planned the unfinished Palace of Justice, of which you and I see the bossed foundations; one family palace is the work of Sangallo the Younger; another (the Falconieri, notable also for giant caryatids at its garden back) owes a river-facing loggia to Barromini. Almost every artist then notable had a hand in St. John of the Florentines, church at the far end; and just off the Via Giulia is a little church, Sant' Eligio degli Orefici, built after plans by Raphael. The arch under which we entered the Via Giulia is the start of an unfinished project of Michelangelo's —the Farnese palace was to have been linked, by a bridge passageway, with the Farnesina, villa or *palazzetto* across the Tiber. The enviable palaces on your left (that is, as you walk with the arch behind you) have gardens which once ran down to the river: today, the embankment cuts them across. The Via Giulia too, being comprehensive, holds one reminder of sin and one of death. Pope Innocent X, in 1655, inserted a (then) modern-style prison, now an interesting museum of criminology, and a church near the arch, Santa Maria della Morte, is or was in the hands of a Confraternity who devote themselves to the burial of the abandoned or murdered dead. On every November 2nd, Augustus Hare says, curious wax figures with reference to death are visited by crowds in the vaults below. Like life, the Via Giulia grows a little less distinct at its far end—it never, as Roman streets go, seems much frequented; nor, though there is nothing against its being a thoroughfare, does it often serve as one—cars enter, but usually to draw up. Do not be disappointed by it, when you first see it: it may be more sombre, to you, than I make it sound. Do not be subdued by the façades; study as many of them as you can. Enter as many courtyards as you dare. At the end of dreadful centuries came a life like this—not that it was perfect.

Far from it, as is shown by Benvenuto Cellini. The rumbustious Florentine goldsmith, off-artist, *entrepreneur* of genius, took up his quarters in the Via Giulia when he had established himself in Rome. St. John of the Florentines to give his countenance and the Raphael church associated with fellow goldsmiths could have been reasons for his choice; as possibly, he simply wanted a good address. The brawls and quarrels which followed him cannot have endeared him to his neighbours. Benvenuto had been born in 1500, eight years after the death of Lorenzo de' Medici the Magnificent. In coming to Rome from Florence, one must remember, he left behind him (though not for ever) what still was, at the time of his move, a more advanced and subtle civilization. The Renaissance, so far, had flourished more on the banks of the Arno than on those of the Tiber. "The progress of the Renaissance in Rome," says Francis Taylor, "is a story quite different from that of Florence or the lesser courts of Italy. It is more stately and less inventive. . . . Because of the elective character of the Papacy, the sense of dynasty so apparent in the Houses of d'Este and Gonzaga took another form. Rome produced few artists or scholars of her own; she had instead the 'receptivity and sterility of all great capitals, spoiled women of pleasure among cities.' But Rome had a unique possession of her own: to her was given the prophetic compensation of long imperial memory. The eternal spiritual and temporal power of antiquity was hers, and to her were drawn irresistibly all of the arts and talents of an alien world."

To the "draw" of Rome was added, for young Cellini, particular reasons to hope for notice. His family for more than one generation had, in Florence, stood high in Medici favour, and the Pope of the Rome he was heading for was a Medici. Leo X, famed *amateur* and collector, second son of the Magnificent Lorenzo, had, indeed, been that very Giovanni who had cracked jokes with Benvenuto's father. Disappointingly, Leo X died before the connection could be exploited. Fortune, however, relented: two years later (1523) a second Medici became Pope, and no less Medician proved his spirit. This former Giulio, nephew of Lorenzo, shows in the portrait of him as Clement VII a resemblance to his secular uncle—the same vigour of attitude, the same handsome-ugly, imperious but generous cast of countenance. Clement VII exceeded Cellini's dreams: unstinting patron, he was to show himself also perceptive friend, invaluable protector.

Benvenuto had set out on the road to Rome with another young man, Tasso, a wood-carver. At Siena Tasso lost his nerve, said his feet hurt, expressed a wish to go home. Next morning, he once again changed his mind—and Benvenuto, who had meantime hired a horse, forgivingly swept him up on to the crupper. "And so, singing and laughing all the time, we made our way to Rome. I was just nineteen then, and so was the century." Twinship with one's century, as I know, somehow gives one the feeling of being hand-in-glove with it, which may make for unavowed extra confidence. Something accompanied Cellini throughout a career in which alliances, otherwise, proved short-lasting. He was luckier than it suited him to admit; ungratefully frequent are his tirades against his "perverse and evil fortune." Admirably was he fit to live in a time which was not only his but in part himself. Aggressive extrovert, he was at his best (effectively) in a competitive maelstrom. Overplaying his hand, arrogantly miscalculating, he retrieved losses by spunk, errors by guile or effrontery. Quick on the draw, he was also a great one for the last laugh—occasions when it was not his are not recorded. My authority on Cellini is Cellini. His memoirs show him violently undecided as to which of two views of himself he wants to present: the maltreated man, or the triumphant one? Enemies compassed him about; if their machinations did for a moment cease he exacerbated them into further action. His virtue, single and unassailable, shines out the more by contrast—he was pure in his attitude to his work. His "I" of the creative moment is impersonal. He stood in awe of the genius in what he wrought; salt-cellar, button, setting for a jewel, nothing could be too small to be great for him —burning for perfection, he never seems to have rested on virtuosity. He dared the line between artist-craftsman and artist when he launched out on the big bronze Perseus which had to be a work of art or nothing. The venture exposed him to every risk, the most dire being that of ridicule: certain as he might be as to inspiration, he was undertaking what had been declared technically impossible—why it had been declared impossible, and for how nearly good a reason, some of his most adequate pages show us. Into his account of the battle of the casting of the Perseus goes his soul. Here is the climax:

> Then suddenly we heard a great noise, and saw a brilliant flash of fire, just as if a thunderbolt had rushed into being in our very midst. Every man of us was dazed by this prodigious and terrifying event, and I still more than the rest. Only when the great rumble and the flashing flame had passed did we dare look each other in the face. Then I saw that the lid of the furnace had blown open, so that the bronze was running over. In the same instant I had every mouth of the mould open and the plugs closed. But perceiving that the metal did not run as freely as it

should, I came to the conclusion that the intense heat had consumed the alloy. So I bade them fetch every pewter dish and porringer and plate I had in the house, nearly two hundred in all; and part of them I threw, one after another, into the channels, and put the rest into the furnace. Then they saw my bronze was really melted and filling up my mould, and gave me the readiest and most cheerful help and obedience. Now I was here; now I was there, giving orders or putting my own hand to the work, while I cried, "O God, who in Thy limitless strength did rise from the dead, and glorious didst ascend to Heaven . . . !" In an instant my mould filled up; and I knelt down and thanked God with all my heart; then turned to a plate of salad lying on a bench there, and with splendid appetite ate and drank, and all my gang of men along with me.

Cellini, if not an example of balanced temperament, led an all-round—might one not say a balanced?—life. The workshop did not bound his horizon; his outside activities were many; poetry and music, he gives us to understand, were his relaxations, though it is hard to see how he had time for them. He enjoyed sport, particularly going after wild duck; he killed at least two men (apart from his exploits in battle) and wounded others. With women he had good times and little trouble; most fun was had with a fierce young model, a pretty virago he enjoyed baiting; he was too shrewd to involve himself with a great lady, nor was he the type for a wast-

ing passion—romance was, anyway, out, with the
Middle Ages. He had reason to complain of the
ambiguity, jealousy, and mischievousness of some
young men. His energy, like his avidity, was tremendous (in the *Life,* he often gives the impression of
being in six places at once) and his physique stood
up to assaults, bangings, and batterings, not to speak
of revolting illness. Once he was knocked out,
though not for long, by being hit in the chest by a
mass of masonry; another time, he cleared off an
indisposition by vomiting up a worm a quarter of a
cubit long, hairy, and covered with green, red, and
black spots—hideous, he tells us. With regard to
society, he was no one's man: he worked to com-
mission, but no one bought him—if a patron was not
fully appreciative, he considered him a dolt, and
showed it; if a patron baulked about paying up, he
was (rightly) furious. In Rome, he moved or rather
thundered about among personalities, cardinals,
princes, generals, who, though in aspect high, wide,
and handsome (having thrown off the narrowness
of the Middle Ages), he knew to be devious. Can-
nily did he observe them, with a view of handling
them. This was a Rome liberated by the Renaissance, if not, moralists might say, improved by it.
The dominating passion was for the costly. As Cellini's fame spread, his masterpieces were competed
for. Gratifying it was to play off the Pope against
the King of France, the King of France against the

Grand Duke of Tuscany, the Grand Duke of Tuscany against the Pope. He was governed by but one loyalty.

The extremeness with which he was what he was makes Cellini expressive of his day, and to an extent its product—to an extent I say, for he had qualities common to other times. His being at once up to the hilt in what went on and calculatingly, warily apart from it makes him, for me, a fitting chronicler of the Rome of the middle sixteenth century—if not, as some may point out, the ideal one. I query whether Renaissance Rome could, by its nature, have produced "the" ideal observer, if by that is meant a disinterested or detached one: there would have been no point in being alive in Renaissance Rome if one had not a finger deep in the pie. Cellini is an impassioned observer. One must, one is told, take him with a grain of salt, which is to say that he exaggerates—enemies say, consistently. Enemies forget that consistency has a virtue: the consistently exaggerated picture is true to a scale of its own, which one comes to recognize. . . . An exceedingly bad patch in his Roman fortunes set in when he fell foul of Pope Paul III, Clement VII's successor. This former Alessandro Farnese had been one of the two cardinals whom Cellini had all but hit with a cannon ball during the battle for Sant' Angelo. "It shall be told in its place," he says of the incident, "how much better it would have been for me if I had killed him." Not content with being tiresome at the time, the Farnese had cunningly waited to settle scores—and a crack of Cellini's, relayed by mutual friends, as to the new Pope's looking, by lamentable contrast with his predecessor, like so many vestments stuffed with straw, had not made the situation better. Paul III had Cellini arrested, charging him with a slaying of which no other person had thought anything but that it had been honourably justified—the man run through with a sword at a street corner being a horrible enemy of Benvenuto's brother's. Paul III thrust Cellini into a stinking dungeon in that very fortress he had defended, condemned him to death, heaped other ignominies on him. Cellini escaped once, only to be recaptured with a broken leg: his account of subsequent agonies makes one sweat—hold was kept upon sanity, however, by the composition of a long, eloquent poem (it may be read in the *Life*). How he extricated himself from the situation, not only alive but with flying colours, several tense, just-credible pages tell. For some time after that he cold-shouldered Rome.

What he did enjoy was being a bombardier. How did it happen that he found himself stationed, alongside the angel, on the topmost platform of Sant' Angelo, laying around him with a cannon? In principle he was firing at the French, who, this year—1527—under command of the Constable of Bourbon but instigated by the Emperor Charles V, had descended on Rome, sacking and burning. (Charles V was the Emperor for whom, nine years later, Pope Paul III laid on that triumphal procession through the Forum.) At the start, the French were contained by the Trastevere, which they rendered an inferno by their atrocities. The French were but part of the rabble of mercenaries, more horde than army, loosed on Rome by the forces of Reformation—the attack, this time, was not only unrestrictedly bloody, it was censorious. Down with the city of iniquities! When, later, the enemy rushed the bridges, the fury spread to main Rome, on the other side: the horrors, rapes, desecrations, torturings, were unspeakable. Clement VII, alas, must be held accountable—he had gone too far, he had reaped the whirlwind. Great was his peril, greater his agitation—the treasures within the Vatican, now including two unparalleled Medici collections (his own and his cousin Leo X's), might at any moment fall into profane hands. Passages connected the Vatican with the massive Castel Sant' Angelo: here the Pope took refuge and had at least some of his treasures brought. Sant' Angelo, once mausoleum of the Emperor Hadrian, now was a military stronghold, the last fort—that it should be manned, and by stalwarts, became essential (ineffectual, so far, had proved the allies called to the Pope's aid). Clement VII bethought him of so far pent-up capacities in his friend Cellini, whose prowess, on finding himself entrusted with no small part (indeed, in his view a major one) of the defence of Sant' Angelo, showed what a psychologist the Pope was.

"There have been times," confesses Cellini, "when I have been more inclined to the profession of arms than to the one of my choice, and with such good will did I give myself up to it now that I did better at it than in my own art." He kept up the firing, he tells us, "with the force and energy of my whole being." Several cardinals and generals blessed him, giving him the greatest encouragement. "Of course, in my impetuous mood I was trying to do the impossible; enough to say that it was through me that the castle was saved that morning. . . . My drawing, my fine studies and my skill in music were all drowned in the roar of those guns; and if I were to tell minutely all the fine things I did in that cruel business, I should strike the world with wonder." Cellini went to his grave, forty-four years later, convinced it was he who had wiped out the Bourbon general. Yet the triumph, looking back at Sant' Angelo, had been for him the sheer lift, the exhilaration, got out of those apocalyptic weeks. Rome, set afire by the enemy, roared to the skies round the artist sky-high beside the angel. "When night came on . . . we who were in the castle—but especially myself, who have always delighted in new experiences—stayed looking on at the extraordinary scene and the conflagration."

"It was pitiful," remarked another observer, "to

see fire consuming the gilded loggias and the painted palaces. . . ."

Rome, by then, one might feel, can hardly have known itself when not burning. Since, it has gone on burning by imitation. Illusory conflagrations mark festal nights—hundreds of thousands of fireworks have gone off from where Cellini's cannon had its emplacement; for us, flood-lighting melts the Forum, making the ruins glow not bright but like embers ever at the point of extinction; elsewhere the miracle is turned upon a fountain, which becomes a dazzle of flamey plumes, or a cascade, which casts sparks rather than spray. The set-alight water, leaping up or down, churning against statues' writhing limbs, beading the basin's lip with fiery bubbles, devours onlookers by reflection and makes façades round it quiver as though being consumed. The art of illumination was in Rome perfected long before there were flood-lights. In the 1850's, William W. Story beheld what was old to the city but new to him: the Easter illumination of St. Peter's.

The first illumination is by means of paper lanterns, distributed everywhere along the architectural lines of the church, from the steps beneath its portico to the cross above its dome. These are lighted before sunset, and against the blaze of the western light are for some time completely invisible; but as twilight thickens, and the shadows deepen, and a grey pearly veil is drawn over the sky, the distant basilica begins to show against it

with a dull furnace-glow, as of a wondrous coal
fanned by a constant wind, looking not so much
lighted from without as reddening from an interior
fire. Slowly this splendour grows, and the mighty
building at last stands outlined against the dying
twilight as if etched there with a fiery burin. As
the sky darkens into intense blue behind it, the
material part of the basilica seems to vanish, until
nothing is left to the eye but a wondrous, magical,
visionary structure of fire. This is the silver illumination: watch it well, for it does not last long.
At the first hour of night, when the bells sound all
over Rome, a sudden change takes place. From
the lofty cross a burst of flame is seen, and instantly a flash of light whirls over the dome and
drum, climbs the smaller cupolas, descends like
a rain of fire down the columns of the *façade,* and
before the great bell of St. Peter's has ceased to
toll twelve peals, the golden illumination has succeeded the silver. For my own part, I prefer the
first illumination; it is more delicate, airy and
refined, though the second is more brilliant and
dazzling. . . . The outline of fire, which before
was firm and motionless, now wavers and shakes
as if it would pass away, as the wind blows the
flames back and forth from the great cups by
which it is lighted. From near and far the world
looks on—from the Piazza beneath, where carriages drive to and fro in its splendour, and the
bands play and the bells toll—from the windows
and loggias in the city, wherever a view can be
caught of the superb spectacle—and from the
Campagna and mountain towns, where, far away
and towering above everything, the dome is seen
to blaze.

Finally, there is the blaze of the moon: nights—
and who knows Rome who has not known one?—
when everything other is outshone. Neons, street-
lights, windows then are no more than spangles at
the bottoms of gutters. The size of the sky, greater
than by day, not so much dwarfs the city beneath it
as gives temerity to its being there. One wonders, in
this negative and dissenting light, not that Rome has
lasted but that it ever began. Though the moon is
nothing but a reflector, it is hard not to think of it
as a scrutiny—here it is, at the full over Rome again,
sceptical as ever. Do not be cheated into expecting
the Colosseum, the Baths of Caracalla, the Forum
to be more wonderful by moonlight; they are less
so—moonlight annihilates history, turning everything into a got-together spectacle for Tonight. It
acts vivifyingly only on living surfaces, grass, trees,
to which it gives texture in lieu of colour; masonry
it reduces to chalk and ink. Strangeness is given, it
is true, to any human who is one's companion—
who is this creature of mauve skin and glittering eye-
balls?—but from architecture miraculousness is
stripped: one is looking at a *décor* or a picture postcard. "See Rome by moonlight!" seems to be an
imperative—I tried, many have, and no doubt you
will. What you see is moonlight. On such walks, I
have never felt further from past people who, from
where I am, have also looked at the moon: the moon
is there, showing me that they are gone.

IV

THE SMILE

To the sun Rome owes its underlying glow, and its air called golden—to me, more the yellow of white wine; like wine it raises agreeability to poetry. One remembers the glow as a constant, the city as a succession of bright distances—there can be blindness to what is harsh or hideous, sprawlingness, raggedness at the edges. There can be days when the eye appeases the ear, diverting it somehow from noisiness—Rome, less excruciating than Paris or Madrid, has inevitably its hell's cauldrons, such as the Piazza Barberini, but I have known those to be endurable, if only for the pleasure of getting out of them: round any corner may be a sudden hush. The February, March, and April I was there, winter was like spring, spring like summer. A mild year, every-body remarked. February, almond and judas trees fluffed the Borghese and other gardens with pink and purple; pavements gave off what (to me, com-ing from the Atlantic) was almost a Mediterranean glare; soil was hard underfoot, and flags out or washing drying flicked at the sunshine like tinted fires. This, a wintry version of what was still in store, acted on me like an extra season grafted into the calendar, a bonus. By April, I found myself thinking twice, round noon, about any ascent of steps—roses began; round me buildings deepened from blonde to honey. While it lasts, such weather seems everlasting.

But there is no constant, rather a range of changes which are extreme, theatrical. (The only neutral I know of is a drained-away day, such as that of my February arrival, when the sky fades over a Rome fatigued and unreal.) There are onslaughts which have the character of reprisals—such as when, under an iron cloud-ceiling, grit begins by blowing in weird puffs, then gales mount up into ferocity, spat-tering bent fountains, clawing at awnings, ruffling the dull Tiber, dementing the shutters on their hooks. My first Sunday, wind wrenched a glass tran-som out of a public building and dashed it on to the street across the way, all but decapitating a pair of lovers. Rome has also an anti-weather which makes for lassitude, through heaviness, or tension—nothing is more ominous than when clouds pile up, fulvous and inky, behind livid buildings on the hills. Thunder grumbles more angrily here than elsewhere. Rain crashes down so hard that it rebounds, making everything dark, clammy, and stuffy indoors or out—there may be Venice-like reflections in the watery tarmac; and rain is to be admired inside the Pantheon, where, falling through the round aperture in the top of the dome, it forms a diaphanous central pillar, running away at the base through the slots cut for it. Otherwise, nothing is so demoralizing, unedifying, and indeed dangerous as a Roman wet day—everything goes slippery underfoot, traffic makes lunges at you half-blindedly, for on streaming windscreens wipers cannot work fast enough. Write such a day off, if you can afford to: settle for a cinema, or, in a corner of a café, puzzle over the blank back pages of a neglected diary. The insides of many churches you deem this an opportunity to visit will be blotted out. As for museums and galleries, those merit better than to be resorts or refuges, surely?

As against that, nothing is more quickly forgotten than a Roman wet day. It vanishes like a quickly retrieved mistake—one which has been, anyway, out of character. Sometimes in the middle of a night I have been wakened by rain stopping: when one has

fallen asleep to it, one misses it. Most often, it is
over in time for sunset—then, pavements steam up
into the long, late rays; in the sunshot aftermath
stone, stucco, and ironwork glisten as though new-
varnished, and the final drip-drops from trees and
balconies flash like trembling prisms before falling.
Colour comes rushing back, to be caught up in this
burst of compensatory brilliance before night-fall.
Air smells of gutters and gardens, sodden newspa-
pers, shellac, refreshed dust. Quite soon, nobody
coming indoors will leave behind them a wet foot-
print. An hour later, rain is a finished story.

How can Rome, with this physical volatility, be
tragic? Enact tragedy, yes, live it out, no. So many
disavowals, inconstancies, changes of face! One
comes to see something climatic about history. In
spite of all the monuments, busts and statues, inscriptions on the arches, I had the sense, often, of
being in a city of oblivion. Or does Rome wear this
carelessness like an outer coat? I doubt it: there can
be a saturation-point with regard to feeling, an
instinctive reaction against memory—could one
wonder, here, if those had been reached? Yet, for
centuries of the generality of people, *was* feeling
more than that of the moment? The gravity, the passion for the conception, the resoluteness that forged
Rome into Romanness, one must associate with the
great few, the minority who stood out against the
undertow—successive legislators, administrators,

writers and orators, campaigners. Those gave
scale to the Roman destiny. Uncompromisingness
created a moral pattern; to be of the *élite* was to
bear its stamp. The rest, the others, being voluble
and fickle were also malleable; to the point required
they could be worked on. Rome knows tragedies,
but they were individual—there is a stone-coldness
about great Roman thought, alone in the warm
weather of the senses. As things went, the worst happened so many times: was there not to come to be
something saving about the general fluidity of the
temperament, its rebounds, its power to throw off
violences and distresses by forgetting them? Often
has fire consumed Rome; it would appear that grief
never has—were history felt, could it be survived?
There have been all but incredible recoveries. The
overall of Rome is the golden glow.

Yet what numbers of visitors Rome has harrowed!
Bursts of eloquence went to show it; one could com-
pile a verse-album of noble dolefulness. The chaos,
the desolation, the fallen glory!—inspired, poets
whipped out their tablets; overcome, amateurs became poets. Unfortunately it does not make one a
poet to lose one's head. Shelley kept his, and therefore soared; Byron pulled out the organ-stops and
performed superbly. But the rank-and-file pages of
our album would consist of stilted hullabaloo, for
the great part in a convention, that of the eighteenth
and early-nineteenth centuries. (I suggest the album

confine itself to the English language.) Sometimes the bard declares himself struck speechless—why was it out of his power to remain so? Were these outbursts spontaneous?—which amounts to wondering, *were* they outbursts? Or were they considered to be "the thing"? The emotion vented was, I believe, genuine; the expression seldom was not laborious. Many of the effusions address Rome, proffering gentlemanly condolence. "Niobe of the nations . . ." To address, one must personify: Rome, distraught widow or injured matron, is perceived to be tearing her honoured grey locks, rolling her eyes, beating her heaving breast—shorn of splendour, bereft of her mighty sons. Never was grief so respectable, never solicitude more lugubrious. *Was* her downfall, however, wholly unmerited? Unhappily, there are those who cannot condole without sounding smug, or at least admonitory. The grotesqueness arises, for me, from this: I cannot imagine anything in the world less like an elderly female, distraught or otherwise, than Rome is. If one must give sex to a city, Rome must be masculine. It seems simpler to speak of the place as "it."

The Forum, I said, leaves one with little to say—I could have as easily said, with nothing. Silence seems the only possible comment on finality. I do not think you or I feel less, but we feel, because more resignedly, more calmly. There is something in anything's being here at all. To the visitors of the Age

of Reason, ruins in themselves can have been nothing fresh—most of them had them at home, took enjoyable carriage drives to view them, domesticated
them in their parks or gardens, or, were they lacking where needed, faked them. They were all for
"interesting melancholy." But the wholesale was different; its thoroughness was unnerving. Rome was
the archetype on which those generations had been
brought up—that it fell they knew, but it had not
really fallen until they saw it. The brutish actuality
of a scene of violence . . . It hit at them; perhaps
they could not forgive it. They reasserted themselves
into declamatory poetry.

They saw, of course, very much more of a mess
than we see now—indiscriminate, tottery, overgrown, less picturesque than painters had led them
to hope. And I take it their sense of decay was added
to by the run-down state of the city round them—
"modern" Rome, one must recollect, underwent pe-
riods of stagnation: blotchy façades, weed-grown
piazze, foetid alleys. The palaces in which they were
entertained (if they had introductions) were dark
as catafalques inside, cobwebby, musty. Setting out
for an evening, our friends drove axel-high through
the ground-mists of the Campus Martius. Many of
them jittered with dread of fever; some loathed
Baroque; many were anti-Popish. Mumbo-jumbo
encompassed them; there were fleas in their beds.
Much of Antiquity could not be got at—carven

doorways, capitals, columns, scraps of inscription, portions of arches had got themselves embedded into the Ghetto, amid flapping black rags and a stinking fishmarket. *Sic transit* . . . They saw it that way.

The ruins have been ruined, you may be told. Stripped bare! Nature had dealt with them tenderly, making them glades inside, forests along their tops —feathery trees dear to Piranesi, showering creepers, bushes, grasses, wild flowers in variety. The flora of Antiquity could be studied, and was; I have handled a volume pretty with tinted drawings, old, hard to come by today, a collector's piece. The Colosseum was bright with flowering weeds which grew nowhere else; legend said they spring from the martyrs' blood. And now—uprooted! Today, the seating-arrangements in the dreadful Colosseum are open to the eye, if that is what interests you. The Baths of Caracalla—why not have left them as Shelley found them, "mountainous ruins," on whose green-shaded slopes he sat writing *Prometheus Unbound?* "This poem," his preface tells us, "was chiefly written . . . among the flowering glades and thickets of odiferous blossoming trees, which are extended in ever-winding labyrinths upon its immense platforms and dizzy arches suspended in the air. The bright-blue sky of Rome, and the effect of the vigorous awakening of spring in that divinest climate, and the new life with which it drenches the spirits, even to intoxication, were the inspiration of this drama." William Story, thirty or so years later, is more botanically specific. "Come," he urges, "to the massive ruins of Caracalla's Baths—climb its lofty arches, and creep along the broken roofs of its perilous terraces. Golden gorses and wall-flowers blaze there in the sun, out of reach; fig trees, whose fruit no hand can pluck, root themselves in its clefts; pink sweet-peas, and every variety of creeping vetch here blooms in perfection; tall grasses wave their feathery plumes out on dizzy and impracticable ledges."

No "monstrous, inform blocks" now offer the climber a lead up the sheer walls. ("When these great pieces fell," goes on William Story, "Rome shook with their thunder, and the people said, 'There is an earthquake.' ") Not a shoot of green mitigates the shock of the vast gauntness. I do not want anything to mitigate the shock—I cannot lament the banishment of Nature. The stripping so bitterly objected to has restored the heavy sharpness of outline proper to a Rome that was not yet Niobe. Here at least is shape, clean as a whistle! Shadow brims up in it, sun colours it. If bushes and creepers still grew here, they would be full of cigarette cartons and bus tickets.

Lamentable, in some eyes, have been the changes. The eyes are those of a small band, the final break-

ers of lances against oblivion. Be aware of the cult
of *Roma Sparita* ("Vanished Rome")—not, in this
case, that of antiquity but the Rome still just, or all
but, within living memory. Those who knew it, or
knew those who knew it still further back, necessarily grow fewer with each season. Some are Roman
born, many are of the colony which comes to feel
itself foreign in name only, others were visitors since
far-off childhood. They are an *élite,* welded together
by a sense of loss, and no less, I felt, by a sense of
guardianship—their memories will be irreplaceable:
this they know, when they honour one with their
conversation. It can be ghostly to be about in the
city in their company, for one feels them to be seeing the now invisible, the swept away, the sacrificed,
the supplanted. The *sparita,* as it is meant and felt,
dates back not much more than a hundred years;
that is to say, it does not take count of vanishings
longer ago than that. It is Rome's yesterday.

Roma Sparita, though in effect an atmosphere,
partly psychic and partly social, has its own distinct, objectifiable topography. It is authenticated:
to see how, visit the Museo di Roma, housed in the
Braschi palace on the Corso Vittore Emanuele, a
stonesthrow from the Piazza Navona. Here hangs a
permanent exhibition—oil and water-colour paintings, etchings, and, in another section, old brown
photographs. No picture has won its way in on sentiment only; each has something to tell. Were these

better paintings, they would I expect be elsewhere; as they are, they hardly could be more speaking. Feeling breathes from them, they are incitements to nostalgia—acting upon one through the mood which begot them, if not through the scenes, objects, or customs they depict. The *sparita,* within these bulky Victorian frames, has the air of existing in a peculiar light, limpid and naïve. Many are the sunsets or glass-clear dusks; noon skies are a sinless, unheated cobalt blue. Early evening shines over a Tiber not yet embanked, in whose reedy reaches youths pole flat-bottomed boats, against the luminous distance of the marshes. Sant' Angelo and the Bernini figures along the bridge have the look of rising from faerylands forlorn. Panniered mules or donkeys, in view of the Colosseum, troop nimbly, with *contadini,* between olive-garden walls. Streets peter out into open landscapes; on spits of gravel under the bridges there are encampments. There opens a slap-happy, colour-splashed, tatterdemalion world of copper pots, yellow and red petticoats, street musicians, trellises, wine-skins, *bambini* burying their faces in hunks of melon.

Bustle returns to markets since driven forth from the sites they cluttered. Brown-and-orange Rome of the jumbled by-streets and ambling riverside looks fruity, a rich, cut-into cake. Yet here also is a domain for the wistful sentiments. The scenes shift; we have also leisure and culture, silences privileged and sedate—waiting-places for carriages, villa gates, dust-softened winding roads on the outskirts, terraces where only a convent bell comes to the ear of the stroller between the statues, glades where the English played cricket, cypressy skylines, unmolested easels propped in the shade. This, we are reminded, was the Rome of the ebullient nineteenth-century "artists," which was to say, painters and sculptors. Flocking hither, from less sympathetic lands, they constituted themselves in their own way a ruling class, with special prerogative and festivals. Unplucking the ties they had worn at home, they gave themselves over to merriment, and artistry. Many were Teutonic or Anglo-Saxon: the on-the-whole mediocrity of their output is, I think, many times atoned for by the vigour they pumped into Roman air. All this overflowing world was at their command; models, waiting to be hired, sat all day in droves on the Spanish Steps, peach-plump or interestingly scrawny, both sexes, all types and ages, got up accordingly, chattering, flashing their eyes and earrings, spitting. The artists, when not cavorting in bands around the Campagna, or making merry on viney *trattoria* terraces nearby the Villa Barberini, or in their studios, were lionized at *conversazioni*. Only the "blackest," most impregnable indigenous Roman society held out, it seems, at that time, against artisticness. The place seethed with amateurs carrying sketchbooks; Augustus Hare organized sketching-parties for ladies, with whose ways he came to be well acquainted—not one would he sponsor unless she carried a shawl; nothing did he not know about damps and chills. Concern for underclad ladies at sunset, in sunless churches or dour museums, characterizes his *Walks in Rome*.

There were inner circles, such as Story's, the Brownings'; friendships, loves, conversations, and inspirations. Those showed less in the Rome of the day, matter more to us—letters, poetry, memoirs immortalize them. I have in mind, more, in dwelling on the *sparita,* more ordinary people whose spirits were also drenched, "even," as Shelley had said, "to intoxication." Or at the very lowest, they were contented. To Rome came the well-to-do in flight from a smoke-greyed England or raw America: industrialism, soul-killing streets, top hats. Romantics, unlike their predecessors of the Age of Reason, they wished Rome in no way other than as they found it —over everything shimmered illusion's veil. Days took on size, from the endlessness of unfrequented ilex avenues to go driving in, shuttered successions of marble rooms, the immensity of the churches to be stood in and galleries to be gazed around, hours of evening by the grey-green river when nothing but distant singing was to be heard, ruins enlarging as the sun sank. And Rome abounded in "characters," such as Beppo of the sidelong, teasing, twinkling black glance and merry quip. Poverty plus quick wits raised a host of jesters.

Now and then, for an instant, the veil thinned. Putrescence forced itself on to notice—phosphorescent fish scales clogging a gutter, rotting fruit rind slimey under the foot, stench from out a palatial doorway. The inverse of this life-lovingness, fecundity, was the shovelling of corpses into a common pit. In the mid-century, there were hints of a pit more dreadful: voiceless imprisonment. Residents and visitors hesitated to probe under the surface of Papal Rome, splendid with ceremonies, processions, given *panache* by the guards. The city's people were under the rigour of ultra-reactionary Papal government, whose excesses good Pius IX himself either could not check or did not know of. Espionage was everywhere; any suspected Liberal walked in danger —secret police interrogatories implemented by torture, engulfment by some virtual oubliette. Repression bore heavily on the press, gagged, and the arts, censored. The theatre, now, was a dressy mockery; the opera was not beyond suspicion—classic *libretti* were subject to safety cuts. "Genius rots here," admits William Story, sombrely, in the late 1850's. He had in mind not the rollicking "artist" set, passports in pockets, safe-guarded foreigners, but his young Roman friends at a standstill, cynical or lethargic. 1870 saw the fetters struck off—long-awaited victory of the Risorgimento: unification of Italy, Rome its capital. Liberation signalized itself by a rush of progress: reorganization, embanking, building. Keen new brooms went into action; civic war was declared against the "backwardness" left by the old *régime*. Alas, the backward was also the picturesque! One could not have it both ways: 1870 saw the start of the vanishing of the now *sparita*. Yet the vanishing was gradual—looking back at it. I know those who found little wrong with the Rome of 1900, 1910. Roman 1920's are, even, by some regretted.

So, look at yesterday in a show of pictures. To me, the exhibition gives off not melancholy but a transferred pleasure—that of seeing what has been loved so well. I cannot sigh for *Roma Sparita;* I have not lost it, for I did not know it. Also, the more I gaze at the exhibition the more I query—is all this, actually, as *sparita* as all that? Much I am shown here is a Rome I continue to come upon round corners. I have wandered into what may be the *sparita* of the future. When I am old in Rome, shall I also mourn? . . . Meanwhile, I move off to study exciting paintings of Garibaldi's battle for the Janiculum, then on down into the Museo di Roma's basement, where are installed the sacredly gorgeous railway coaches, date 1858, made in Paris for the last of the mobile Popes, Pius IX.

It becomes Rome to be open to the sun, open to the eye. One rejoices in positive spaces, like giant ballrooms, connected by corridors of perspective.

The longer the distances to look down, the greater the pleasure. This is realized by "Sistine" Rome, which, extending from the Esquiline to the Quirinal, also to the Pincian, is so called because it was evolved by Pope Sixtus V (1585–1590). One marvels at how much this inspired man carried out within so short a reign—one must think, he rushed into being, once come to power, what he had had in mind most of his life. Also this particular time of his accession presented him with an idealist's opportunity: Rome, devastated in 1527 by the Imperial rabble armies and the incendiarism witnessed by Cellini, cried out for reconstruction and re-embellishment. Restoration was needed by pride laid low. By no means all of the city had been wiped out—note the happy escape of the Via Giulia so near the embattled riverfront, the early-Renaissance palaces of the Campus Martius, and churches everywhere—but all Rome had felt the blow to morale. The Esquiline-Quirinal area would appear to have been among those surviving, for Sixtus V began by sweeping away mediaeval streets which, otherwise, would have baulked his project. (He had what is yearned for by city-planners: absolute, ungainsayable authority.) Sistine Rome, therefore, did not replace earlier glories gone up in smoke; it was an addition, eloquent and timely.

Since 1527, there had begun and ended the lengthy Council of Trent; with, as outcome, re-defi-

nition and affirmation of the Church of Rome's
lately challenged authority. Charles V's somewhat
guarded attempt to gain hearing for the forces of
Reformation, from whom he might, in return, again
be glad of support, had been foiled at the outset. It
did emerge, however, that the strengthened Vatican
must be above reproach; laxities and resultant
scandals were not any longer to be countenanced.
Secular magnificence, accorded, was to link with
spiritual austerity. Sixtus V, as Pope, perfectly answered this fresh requirement: only in one particular did he not conform. Rome of the late sixteenth
century and of the century to follow was the Rome
of the Counter-Reformation; with that, the architectural association is Baroque—Sixtus V still thought
on other lines; his tastes preserved the classicism of
the Renaissance. He was for the stretching, the ae-
rial, and the uphill. Planning, he launched streets as
one might let off arrows. He so built as never to be
oppressive. Sistine Rome is to be thought of as a
beautiful, geometrical spider's-web, spun from hilltop to hilltop. The web dips in the middle, but without slackening or losing pattern. On the Esquiline
side, it takes in two great pre-existing churches:
these, we are caused to see from as many angles and
distances as possible.

Sistine Rome has stood up, where need be, to
modern pressure. Organically part of a living city,
it has in places assented to business centres, shop-

ping-vortexes, and streets widened for heavy commercial traffic. But in what still is the greater part, little of the character has been forfeited. Sistine layout survives where buildings do not; elsewhere, tracts seem in a conspiracy to remain as they are, at whatever cost—I fancy, sometimes a high one. And, walking through the area's whole extent, one finds oneself ending as one began, in considered spaciousness.

You begin upon an elating, enormous plateau, the sun-polished Piazza di San Giovanni in Laterano—having ascended to it (let us imagine) by a street of the same name, from the Colosseum. You enter the *piazza* at one corner—each time I did so, I caught a breath. You behold the obelisk, highest in the world, oldest in Rome, whose shadow, were you to stay and watch, could be seen to move round the day like a single clock-hand. The openness you confront is in shape irregular, being cut into by the Lateran Palace, now museum, which protrudes from and hides the flank of the church. One of the church's impressive entrances is in an enclave between the palace and the baptistry. San Giovanni itself, Rome's second cathedral, acts, from here, chiefly, on the imagination—its major portico faces another way, and seems to me to belong to another picture. . . . The piazza's other side is bounded by a line of assorted buildings: rival cafés invite you. Here and there occur gaps which are heads of streets—Via Merulana, the first you come to, you take.

Merulana, today somewhat drab, was a master-piece lead-through of Sixtus V's. Framed at its end, small with distance but nearer with every step, is a segment of Santa Maria Maggiore, and the wonder-ful church as a whole waits to reward you. I suggest that, having reached it, you walk straight through —in at the near door, out again at the far. (By "straight" I do not, as you will understand, mean hurriedly, blindly, or disrespectfully: how long you stay, *en route,* and how much you absorb, this time, of Santa Maria's glimmering marble interior is for you to say. Simply, I mean "straight" in terms of the walk.) The church is an elevated island in a sea of traffic—emerging from it, standing in the doorway, you gaze across into the Piazza dell' Esquilino, set back in a comparative hush. Out of the centre-back end of the Esquilino opens a street: yours—now you have ahead of you Sixtus V's lengthiest arrow-shot. In spite of name-changes along its course, this street is unbroken in continuity, for exactly how great a distance I cannot say. It can hypnotize by its scenic risings-and-fallings, its never-deflectedness, its unendingness. Beginning as the Via Depretis, it be-comes (after one busy intersection) the Via delle Quattro Fontane; finally, after its dip down into the Piazza Barberini it goes up the Pincian hill as Via Sistina. Where that comes out, at the Trinità dei

Monte, you are again at a height. The greater part of Rome stretches below you: you have been carried to the head of the Spanish Steps.

Another plateau tops Rome's highest hill, the Quirinal. This area, though it may be reached from below, is best entered from the Via delle Quattro Fontane, at the point marked by the "Moses" fountains. Turn down the corridor which is the Via del Quirinale—discreet, full of official silence, often empty but for the pacing sentries, overlooked by the half-shuttered flank of the palace; with, across the way, Bernini's oval gem of a church, Sant' Andrea (not in the Sistine picture), together with a stretch of the formal gardens to which much of this high ground is given over. Though you see ahead of you, there is to be a suddenness about the entire burst of sky, Rome, and space which is the Piazza del Quirinale—which is why I say, enter at one corner. This is another "ballroom," launched out, at an angle, over the city. On its outer sides, there is nothing but a low balustrade.

The great floor tips downward (which, now I think of it, would be a dancing problem). At the top, gaze fixed on far-off St. Peter's, is the Palazzo del Quirinale—long, low, the façade keeps its initial simplicity, though Sixtus V's successors did what they could to variegate or adorn it, adding an end tower, a Bernini portal. The building is of a yellow no other Roman yellow approaches; it has a melon underglow. This *piazza* atones by colour, and dazzlingness, for what it lacks in order—as to the latter, it is inferior to the Laterano. Awkwardly close together, its major ornaments look like objects dumped, at random, out on the floor during a house-cleaning. They comprise two colossal statues, one obelisk, one fountain with extra-capacious basin. The Dioscuri—Castor and Pollux, each with his rearing steed—were, at the outset, brought by Sixtus V from the nearby remains of the Baths of Constantine, and here "placed" with the usual Sistine flair, their bases the ideal distance apart. So far, so good. But a later Pope, less inspired, fancied the fountain dug from the Roman Forum, and succeeded in having its scalloped granite lip shoved up as close as possible to the Dioscuri, on the palace side. The effect, still bearable, may be seen in the painting of the Piazza del Quirinale by Gaspar van Wittel (1647–1736). Nagel's guide-book attributes the error to Pius VII, but that Pope's dates were 1800–1823, so we have as counter-evidence the Van Wittel picture. Pius VI (1775–1799) is charged—in *this* case, dependably?—with the obelisk. His eye having lit upon one to spare, in the Mausoleum of Augustus, he had it hauled here, and caused its substantial pediment to be wedged between the bases of the twin statues. You cannot, the good man may

have thought, go wrong with an obelisk. You can.
Monumental chaos remains a monument to inability
to let well alone.

These and other not always happy Papal atten-
tions and additions to the Quirinal are accounted
for by its having been the summer residence of the
Popes, up to the changes of 1870. From then, up to
the deposition of Italy's King Umberto, it was, as we
all know, the Royal palace; since 1946, it has been
the residence of the President of the Italian Republic. Indifferent, as must be any great theatre, to the
changing portent of dramas played upon its stage,
it continues to offer setting for ceremonials. What I
think of, when I look at the yellow palace, is, that
it was here, while there were still only the Dioscuri,
alone in colossal innocence under the windows, that
Sixtus V died. God is praised in His works, praised
in the instrumentality He has given man. Sixtus V
brought Rome's extravagant distances and bewilder-
ing contours into a discipline which is beautiful. Art
harmonizes. His *piazze* add wonder and size to daylight by containing it—so do lakes to water—and
in the joy set up one's spirit dances like David before the Lord. Nor was this all; he re-erected obe-
lisks, bestowing them where the Rome reincarnating
itself beneath his eyes came to require that they
should be, and arriving, under God, each time and
in whichever place (Piazza San Pietro, Piazza del

Popolo, Piazza di San Giovanni in Laterano, or where you will) at miraculous rightness in the relation between the height reached and the space dominated. (The nerve-cracking tensity of the operation, the actual getting into the perpendicular of the huge thing, hauled to the spot, recumbently waiting, is borne in by the St. Peter's story or legend—the enjoined silence, death to be the penalty for the onlooker who so much as caught a breath or whispered a word, the sailor's irrepressible cry of warning, the wetted ropes. . . .) Further, Sixtus V brought in or rather brought back water, partly repairing, partly diverting one of the many derelict ancient aqueducts of the Campagna, so that flow resumed from the hills around Palestrina to feed Sistine-Roman fountains, twenty-seven in all. The play of aquatic plumes in front of St. Peter's, triumphantly misting the colonnades, is the most spectacular of his living memorials (water lives, stone not) but the naïve Quattro Fontane are the most intimate: the laughed-at Moses statue, the beaming lions commemorate a metaphorical striking of the rock—here the water-giver stood watching the first gush. He had been of humble birth, a country lad, Felice Peretti: the name was his throughout his years in the Church, till old age saw him Sixtus V. The waters piped into this part of Rome are therefore called the Acque Felice: it is likely that the people in general honoured him more for this benefit than for any other.

There is a Rome on which the sun either never has shone or shines no more. A traffic tunnel has been bored through the Quirinal, for instance, deep down under the gardens of the palace—trees are up above at a great height, like those which sprouted atop the ruins, as your taxi roars into the tunnel's mouth. Also there is the Metropolitana, the city's pretty, *manqué* underground railway, designed, in the first place, to carry inrushing visitors to Mussolini's projected exhibition, the ambitious "1942." That particular rush of visitors remained phantom. Guidebooks, in their "information" sections, are as reticent on the subject of the Metropolitana as they are, elsewhere, about the Aurelian Wall—for, I imagine, the same reason: as things turned out, neither made history. But I was always fond of the Metropolitana, its infrequent trains in which the handfuls of passengers seemed to like the ride and be having a good time, its booking-halls, passage-ways, and platforms glossy with butter-coloured marble and immaculate, I am sure, as any in Moscow. You could drop into the lull of the Metropolitana at several points, and it ended by cantering out into open country.

Deeper underground, just outside the Porta Maggiore, is something different. You cross a maze of railway-tracks, then descend a steep, thirty-foot

flight of steps, to enter the Basilica Sotterranea—
which, its past being still uncertain, has so far been
accorded no other name. It is ancient, and its condition suggests that it was abandoned and sealed
up after not many years of use. Moreover, it then
disappeared from memory: for centuries the people
over its head had not a notion that it existed. In
1917, on April 21st (Rome's birthday), it was blun-
dered upon, and all but into, by workmen busy with
their picks on this shunting-yard of the Rome-Naples
line. One thinks of a cathedral at the bottom of the
sea, but that the building is pagan, the sea is earth,
unmurmuringly pressing against the walls. The form
of this mysterious basilica is perfect; the central
nave, with a high apse at the end, has over it a
lofty barrel ceiling. The ceiling, the upper parts of
the walls, the pilasters, and the insides of the arches
are decorated with stucco reliefs, mythological
scenes, single figures, motifs, within frameworks of
slender mouldings or scrolls. For the lightness
which is their livingness, there are no words—one
of the groups on the ceiling, a winged rape, might
be a Tiepolo in plaster. It seems they were painted,
once; colour has perished, leaving behind it in yel-
low-pearl the enduring fragility of the stucco. Dif-
fused lighting (never, in all Rome, better than here)
causes limbs, draperies, wings, columns, masks,
candelabra to gleam towards you, outlined by shallow shadows. Yet the interior, for all the golden ac-

centuations given it, is as a whole pallid as a wan evening. Hollowed down to the depth it is, this basilica never knew or was intended to know daylight, other than the one shaft projected into it by means of the aperture in the ceiling—closed when the place was abandoned for evermore. A floor drain under the former opening reminds one that here, as in the Pantheon, from time to time stood a column of rain. That this was a banqueting-hall, that it was a tomb, that it was the meeting-place of a religious sect has, in turn, been suggested. The third suggestion, some instinct favours—something went on down here other than eating-and-drinking or lying dead. Symbolism in some of the decorations gives reason, it seems, to connect the place with the Neo-Pythagoreans: this I do gladly.

The Subterranean Basilica (I imagine, because of the cost of lighting it so sublimely) is open only two days a week. I recollect those days as Mondays and Thursdays, but that should be checked on: all things change, and it could be annoying to embark over the railway tracks for nothing.

Under the church of San Clemente (which, already two layers deep, is on the Via di San Giovanni in Laterano) you may penetrate into the deep-down sinister temple, with altar, dedicate to the cult of Mithras. This dates back to the second century B.C.; its arc of rocky ceiling is moist and rough-hewn— the place gave me the creeps. And from Rome's below-ground I must not omit the Catacombs—though I could, for those officially shown are outside the city, and perhaps I should, for they are not my subject. The most extensive and fully organized are those of San Callisto, some way out along the Appian Way. There are indeed others along that route, as a thirsty walk showed me: for me it was past *trattoria*-hour when I found that each promising sign-board to which I sped invited me to more sombre pleasures. A visit to or rather descent into the Catacombs is among the "musts" of a sight-seer and the duties of a Christian, and very rightly. Non-Christian sight-seers may give rein, for all I know, to unavowed necrophilia—why these burial-warrens which sheltered, at epochs critical for our faith, the mortal guardians of immortality *should* give off such a reek of death, such physical dreadfulness, cannot be clear to me. Early Christianity, spiritually a Resistance movement, as an organization had the technique, pattern, and one may assume the esoteric vocabulary adopted by other such movements since; like Resistance workers in the occupied countries, long-ago Christians, from time to time, strategically "went underground"—literally they did so here. It may be that the capacity to react to the Catacombs I normally should have had, had I come fresh to them, was exhausted, long in advance, by over-stress on childish imagination. Religio-historical romances, whose protagonists were juvenile persecuted Christians, were not only handed to me; I lapped them up. But, as they accumulated, I came to spot the imprimatur of one or another publisher statedly propagating religious knowledge. Religion one cannot be set against, if one has it in one, but forever I was set against propaganda. However noble the motive, secular or sacred, I will not have powder in the jam. My shrinking distaste for the Catacombs is another matter—claustrophobia plus terror of getting lost (though one could not, in fact, be more ably shepherded). The Vatican, to which San Callisto belongs, allocates visitors, according to nationality, to wise guides in each case speaking their charges' language—the one time I ever did stray behind, I panicked head-on, round the first corner, into nothing worse than the head of a file of Germans, who, faces red-raw under bobbing tapers, were forging towards the conclusion of their tour. The Vatican had not then instituted electric lighting (it since has), therefore any abrupt halt, gesture, or turn-around sent fine grease from one's taper on to one's neighbour's clothes; on to one's own fell similar rain from one's neighbour's taper. Flame-points, wavering fitfully into the arched niches, played on what might or might not be powdered bones. Beatitude, however, comes from the wall paintings in the low, cramped chapels where the Christians worshipped: these are pictures like sunrises on the darkness —a Resurrection of Lazarus, a Eucharist. . . .

170

So near are they in feeling to what they show, so joyful and fervent is the depiction, that the inspired brushes might have been children's. The overtone is a floating and lucent yellow; the distinct other colours are those of morning, when its unearthly earliness gives promise of more than an earthly day. Elsewhere, what I can never stand is the recumbent statue of St. Cecilia. I must stress what the guides, who are cleric-scholars, are scrupulously insistent in pointing out—that the Catacombs' interestingness extends beyond Early Christian association. A respectable secular reason for the visit would be, study of burial-customs. Above San Callisto, in a laid-out garden, butterflies are at liberty for a surprising number of months in a Roman year; now and then a lizard darts over the sunny gravel. This is life, upon which one looks one's last while waiting for one's fellow nationals to assemble in order to "go down."

Aboveground, pleasures and palaces . . . One or another desire or curiosity shaped my courses for runs of days. The pursuit through Rome of one artist, such as Bernini, or tracking down of vestiges of some epoch, or search for the answer to some enigma exciting or troubling to my mind, but not, it seemed, to anyone else's—anything of that sort could be enough to keep me zigzagging about the city, not so much at random as might appear. What meant little yesterday could be a clue today. A hunt, with the disregard for everything else that it sets up, is itself pleasure. Nor does one know where one may not be landed up—I got to know Rome as a hunter gets to know country. Equally, there were moods, which I gave way to. A relationship cannot stand still; there are phases and developments and it may be setbacks in one's having to do with a place, particularly if it be Rome. As for going about, I know I do not care for being conducted, for more than a few steps or a few minutes, however well. Nothing, that is say no one, can be such an inexorable tour-conductor as one's own conscience or sense of duty, if one allows either the upper hand: the self-bullying that goes on in the name of sight-seeing is grievous. Fatigue, rebellious distaste due to satiation, may ruin Rome for you—should *you* lay Rome in ruins over again? Enjoy yourself, I say—having in mind that there is always the matter of learning how to. This book is not even my footnote to your guide-book; it is my scribblings on the margins of mine. I claim to be little help to anyone else.

It seemed to me hopeless to make a methodical round of all Rome's churches. I admired many simply for their façades; I entered, and very often, the same few, and those less on account of the merits for which they might be starred than because they drew me. Some meant journeys, others grew dear through familiarity from being in parts of Rome

where I often found myself. Those in which I spent
most time were, Santa Maria in Cosmedin, down by
the Tiber, not far from the foot of the Aventine; San
Gregorio, overlooking the street of that name, which
runs under a flank of the Palatine to the Arch of
Constantine; Santa Sabina, on top of the Aventine;
Santa Maria in Domnica (or, della Navicella) on top
of the Caelian, with in front of it the small marble
ship; Santa Maria Maggiore; St. Peter's; Sant'
Andrea al Quirinale; San Giovanni a Porta Latina,
near the gate of that name, peacefully shaded by an
enormous cedar; San Pietro in Vincoli, on the Esquiline near the Via Cavour, up alleys and flights of
steps, containing the Michelangelo Moses. I went
into more others than I can number; I name only
those I cannot forget. Three (each, it happens,
unique in beauty) are set apart by their hiddenness
—these are "secret" churches, to be sought as one
seeks for a cabinet's secret drawer: Santi Quattro
Coronati, back behind two deep courtyards, themselves led to by out-of-the-way streets, uphill off the
Via San Giovanni, on your right as you walk from
the Colosseum; ancient Santa Prassede, darker inside than most, tucked away off the Via Merulana
at the Santa Maria Maggiore end; and Santa
Costanza, circular, having within it Rome's oldest
known Christian, also most lyrical, mosaics. Santa
Costanza lies back of another church, Sant' Agnese
fuori le Mura, whose claims it (for me) unfairly

eclipses; the two are in an enclave off the populous
Via Nomentana. A "horror" church is Santo Stefano
Rotondo, on the Caelian close to the Navicella: it
has frescoes, photographic in detail, of unspeakable
tortures suffered by Christian martyrs. Too much
more has happened since last I saw them, in the days
of my youth; this time the church, in a state of pro-
longed repair, was closed—should it perhaps remain
so? One which, within, resembles a music-room,
pretty, secular-looking (but for its apse mosaics),
and a shade prim, is Santa Cecilia in Trastevere:
this marks the site of the saint's home and somewhat
inhuman young married life, and one still sees her
atrium, now a courtyard quartered into beds of vir-
ginal lilies. She is not, for some reason, my favourite
saint, but the place offers pleasant shelter from
Trastevere dust-storms.

Many Baroque façades tend to run into one in my
memory—wrongly, for no two are really alike. In
retrospect, I cannot distinguish between (for instance) Sant' Andrea della Valle, San Marcello,
Sant' Agostino, Santa Maria della Vittoria, San
Carlino alle Quattro Fontane, though I could tell
you the site on which each is found. Sant' Ignazio
(just off the Corso Romano) I would not fail to
identify, for this reason—the tiny *piazza* it commands is architected in elegant unity with the
church's frontage: here is Rome's most perfect
little outdoor "drawing-room"—as apart from ball-

room—in which, at a restaurant table under an awning, one may while away hours of noon or evening. (A major drawing-room is the Piazza del Popolo.) In the main, my liking was wedded to what is simple —such as Santa Maria della Pace's semi-circular portico, on the Campus Martius. Exception, the glorious virtuosity of Sant' Agnese in Agone, Borromini's façade on the Piazza Navona, dome flanked by pillared *campanili,* doorway sadly blocked from the eye by the "Rivers" fountain. In much of Rome one is hampered, in the taking-in of effect, by crowdedness; seldom is one seeing from far away. How immense the gain may be if one can and does, how enhanced may be noble theatricality, is shown by San Giovanni in Laterano—which, largely masked, as we saw, from the side *piazza,* launches its eighteenth-century "main" portico into other air, statue-topped, at the head of ascents of lawns to ascents of steps. Visible for miles, this is one of Rome's dominant silhouettes.

One Roman pleasure, I found, is the holiday from Rome to be had in gardens. Apart from the Pincian and the Borghese, many are open to you and me— public. Private they formerly were, and they still seem so. Ownership now goes to whoever loves them. Nothing is stone in them but the benches, the fountain-basins, the statues mysteriously located in glades, by grottoes, or at the turns of leafy serpentine walks. Your few living companions are in worlds of their own—lovers, fingertips touching, pause by the pools seriously to contemplate their reflections, as though being photographed; old people sit in dignity in the sun; infants totter and children play with an absorption which keeps them all but silent. Inky are the caverns of ilex shadow; wire tunnels are clambered over by ivy. The flowerbeds may be sparser than they were, or the lawns more worn, but a privileged tranquillity is everywhere—sometimes a path is the way to a small viewpoint balustrade with a large outlook, come upon by nobody else. Such a garden is that of the Villa Celimontana, on the Caelian—the main gate is next-door to Santa Maria in Domnica. Celimontana, now, is the headquarters of the Italian Geographical Society, who have put the villa itself to some learned use, maintain the surroundings, and are your hosts. The gardens extend some way down the hillside; through them you can make a short-cut from the Navicella to S. S. Giovanni e Paolo, escaping nudges from motor cars on the road proper, though thereby, also, missing the rose-red Arco di Dolabella. Corresponding enchantment, across Rome, is to be found in the Villa Sciarra (or Wurts) gardens, halfway up the Janiculum: among bowers of camellia and oleander are lively aviaries. Further along the Janiculum, where the hill rises steeply behind the Palazzo Corsini (now a gallery), are the Botanical Gardens—large, unkempt for the greater part, lush with

forgotten overgrown specimens, here and there
swampy with errant waterways. Scale the mossy
terraces, and the crumbling staircases in which some
steps are beginning to wobble—whether these gardens are "open" remains ambiguous; I only know
that nobody turned me out, and that they provided
a consolation for my failure to enter (it seems that
this *is* impossible) the nearby Orti which were
Queen Christina of Sweden's famed academic
groves. High upon the Capitoline are the garden-
plots which replace the vanished Temple of Jupiter
and, still better, the fronded enclosures or bright
parterres within and around the Palazzo dei Con-
servatori—to reach those, you must buy your way
through the museum. What many people remember
about the Aventine is the magnificent, iron-plated
locked gate through whose keyhole you obtain the
keyhole-shaped, minute view of St. Peter's. But elsewhere the hill is more generous: alongside Santa Sabina is the gladelike Parco Savello, garden in feeling,
with nothing beyond its parapet but sky. I associate
the Savello with singing birds, aisles of slender trees,
and reposefulness—here in so green a space, at so
great a height, above Rome. In the south of the city,
near the Aurelian Wall, between the sedate walled
streets headed respectively for the Latina and San
Sebastiano gates, is a garden-park containing a
columbarium. The only accessible gardens I did
not care for are those known as the Oppio, which,

on the Esquiline, facing the Colosseum, overlie Nero's Golden House—these *have* a "municipal" air; the gravel is dusty and the flowers are garish, the meandering little fences are archly rustic, and the bald scene has as its only features, apart from remains of the Baths of Trajan, brickwork cages, each heading a shaft through which light is filtered into the halls below.

The proper, more sounding name of the Golden House is the Domus Aurea. Unlike the pattern *domus* we have discussed, it was not strong in domestic associations: we see what are said to have been the private apartments of Nero and Poppaea, his lovely consort, but the good-humoured creature's share in this vast establishment was limited, and her days were numbered. Whether the circumstances of her death were or were not as by some reported, I leave open: calumnies stuck to Nero like sackfuls of feathers to a tarred man. He made an exhibition of himself, owning to art gone wrong—a mistake which infuriates the British on account of the embarrassment it causes them, but infuriated the Romans pure and simple: the Greeks, whom he always yearned for, were touched. At home the Emperor, more sincerely loathed for his vain aspirations than his effective cruelties, was doomed to incur what is worst of all, the longlasting rancour of captive audiences. The Domus Aurea, as a carried-through

project, seems to have been his one entire success—
at last, he is said to have said, a house fit to live in!
Can one wonder that it was not forgiven him?
Rome's nearest to a Xanadu pleasure dome, it did
not survive the tyrant's abject death: demolition of
the upper floor of the palace, then denudation, followed by entombment, of the formerly still more
fabulous under-structure (all that, disentombed,
today remains to be shown) were part of the pro-
gramme of retribution by which Nero's Flavian successors made a successful bid for popular favour.
Nor was what was done enough: the Flavians, in a
burst of imperial *largesse*, built baths for the people
over the new-made mound, and allowed, if they did
not cause, leaks to drip through. On painted vaultings, walls, and pavilioned ceilings, mustiness and
erosion soon had their way.

Today, you enter the Domus Aurea, through the
horrible little forefront of rustication, as you might
a cave-dwelling—once, remember, the sunstruck
glitter of its roofs was a magnet to ships coming up
the Tiber. The Domus Aurea, one must also grasp,
was but in part a dwelling; it was a domain, a project, a Versailles-like conception of holding court.
To envisage its size and its stretching opulence, its
knitting of the Esquiline with the Palatine by a system of gardens, corridors, porticoes, and subsidi-
ary ornamental buildings, many reflected into the
lake in the hollow where now is the Colosseum,

needs an act of faith—so completely has everything been expunged. Moreover, nothing within miles of being so beautiful, if only where beauty is in effrontery, supplanted it—with the speculative exception of the now all but equally vanished temple of Rome and Venus. I query, were its successors morally better? Titus's Arch vaunts the reduction to dust of Jerusalem by *force majeure;* disgusting popular spectacles in the Colosseum must have degraded and brutalized far more people than did the vices, by nature fairly exclusive, whose jewelled settings had guarded doors, or languors in scented arbours sunk deep in groves.

Irretrievably damaged by hatred, shorn, voided, made phantom and rendered null, the Domus Aurea has not even power to stir up regret for a silenced rhapsody (of whatever quality). Stains blotch the surrounds of paintings themselves to be guessed at rather than seen; calcinated appear the alcoved chambers into which arc-lamps protrude their glare; the halls, dank, are over you like great soiled tents. Where there are gashes of sickly daylight, they fall on floors which, deadened under one's foot, are glossed by a perpetual sweat. War or time could have accomplished this same work—but it happens that neither *was* the enemy. I could choke with anger against censoriousness, its cautious vengeances, its ungodly claim to the right to judge. I look up an air-shaft at ferns growing between me and the sky. Though it tries the nerves, I walk through the place alone— *"Orgee, orgee, orgee!"* once giggled one of the guides, bucktoothed, conscientious, scuffing as he jumped like a buck rabbit. A guide-book you do require: Miss Robathan is, here, as lucid as she was in the Forum. I could not be long in the Domus Aurea had I not in mind its posthumous triumph. Known of by hearsay, perhaps explored, through inlets, by adventurous children, it was finally penetrated by adventurous painters: Raphael and his pupils discovered themselves to be in a wondrous mine. Inspired, excited, rigging up scaffolding, fixing lanterns, the young men fell furiously to work, copying the murals. Sense of event made them sign their names down here. (The murals were more distinct than they now are: it must be admitted that the artists, tearing open as much of the Domus Aurea as they knew how to, let in weather which wrought havoc: what had been preserved to a point, till then, deteriorated rapidly from then on.) Back again on the contemporary surface, which was the Roman-Renaissance princely art-market, the discoverers brandished their finds in the faces of their patrons: thus were engendered (or re-engendered) those decorations in the style to be known as "the grotesque." Aesthetic frivolities swarmed, like genii out of long-stoppered bottles, back again into the sun of favour. See, as a little example, in the Castel Sant' Angelo, the miniature corridor and the Papal bathroom.

The lost house had more to deliver up. In 1506 some further explorer waved his torch round an octagonal hall, where, among the uncertain crowd in the frescoes, Hector forever bade farewell to Andromache. But it was not the heroic pair who made the intruder start, stop, try to steady his torch. What had been come upon was the Laocoön.

Rome holds in its keeping more than one masterpiece of illusion. Loveliest of those which remain intact is the Empress Livia's painted garden, an additional wonder of the world. A flower-fringed wood, with vague hills undulating behind, this first encompassed an oblong room in Livia's country villa at Prima Porta: not long ago the sylvan scene was transferred to the walls of a room of the same proportions, built for it in the Museo Nazionale. Neighboured in the museum by the modish *domus* decorations we once spoke of, this blue-green eternity of Livia's should be visited on a different, less banal day—one does not merely look at it, one becomes enclosed in it. In these young woods, diaphanous, not more dense than thickets, everything is ardent and fresh-growing, yet drenched as by dew with all time's mystery. Branches and the air between them are alive with birds, and wild doves and finches and others have taken courage and perched

on the trellis, nearer the eye. Gaps in the trellis give
on a strip of greensward between it and the parapet
—which, though it runs all the way round, keeping
back the wood, never is monotonous, for its tracery-
patterns change and it has embrasures. The one tree
framed within each embrasure is, you will note, of a
species rarer (that is, in Italy) than are those min-
gling together in the wood. Near an exotic pine a
rabbit has got in, as rabbits do. The apples and
oranges ripening are few as yet, though enough to
weigh down the still-slender boughs; the flowers
grow, also, not in too great or anonymous profusion
—there is a touch of identity to each as it rests on
the bush, leans from the spray, or springs from the
stem. The wood recedes, as in life, into veils of
atmosphere: everything in the forefront is in stereo-
scopic closeness to you—the veining of leaves, co-
rollas' uneven or dinted petals, the moulded, tipped,
and directed feathers composing the characteristic
plumage of each bird. Elsewhere, only in poetry
could there be such verisimilitude. There is not a
breeze, but the greenery has a look of not perfect
stillness: animate, it must breathe.

I visited Prima Porta: a friend and I and her
cocoa-coloured, aristocratic dogs climbed the slope
to where Livia's villa was—two women paying a
morning call on a third, gone (though not quite)
as were her surroundings. We looked down into
what we had expected—a shell left open, after its

excavation, to convince the hopeful that there *is* nothing more, now. Having wanted to see the first site of the magic wood, the exact locality of its original holding of its sway, I was satisfied. Prima Porta was, in the Empress's time, the first main stop (I imagine, for changing horses) on the Via Flaminia's course from Rome to the north. Round here, the highway dips through wonderful country, on which Nature has showered numerous woods—why did Livia, who had only to go to her door and look out, or lace on stouter sandals and take a walk, choose to encase herself in a painted one? We know who she was, Augustus's wife, the new Roman Empire's First Lady. But what was she?

Anyone interested in watching women deal with the situations in which they find themselves must have been interested by watching Livia. Observed she was. The slight scandal attendant on her divorce from T. Claudius Nero and rush, forthwith, into marriage with Augustus connected with her having been pregnant at the time: that a lady in her condition should brave the law courts then haste, anew, to a bridal bed was considered indelicate; moreover the child with which she was great was not unnaturally rumoured to be Augustus's, though T. Claudius Nero, gentleman to the last, was not to be shaken in his claim to paternity: legally, the boy Drusus remained his. If the boy were indeed Augustus's, what irony—for Livia, once into her second

marriage, bore no more children. That Augustus
could be a father was manifest in the form of the
awful Julia, begotten by him on his irreproachable
first wife, Scribonia, since then divorced for Livia's
sake. For Livia, this man with an unprecedented future opening before him risked what, at that junc-
ture, was all-important: his name for integrity—
battles the youthful Triumvir had won; all the more
it behoved him to be above one battle, that of the
passions. If Livia did not impassion this formal Roman (which, betweentimes, he might have rebelled
against or mistrusted) she must have pleased him,
subtly, deeply, entirely, and as never before, which
sounds less dangerous but may be more so. She
won him, and she kept him. Augustus Caesar, with
his exaltation of lineal descendancy, his conviction
that he should found a dynasty, needed a son no less
than, later, did Napoleon. Both career-emperors
were in the same predicament, locked with former
mistresses into barren marriages. Napoleon put
away Josephine; Livia stayed the course.

When history seems to repeat itself, the centuries
between characters disappear. Apart from circumstance, how much had they in common, the vulnerable Josephine, the adroit Livia? Both had a gift for
interiors: women's charming rooms not only relax
the warrior but ease the confederates brought
home for informal but it may be decisive talks.
Lightly flattering, teasingly discreet would be the

185

conversation of the syren now ensconced as hostess. Malmaison outside Paris, that idyll-setting, with its long couches and little chairs, windows on to the garden, bric-a-brac, draperies classic yet ethereal (what might not Livia have done with muslin!) we see as it was; Livia's intimate house on the Palatine, with its cool courtyard, today is in many ways as it was not. Yet we have a clue as to how it was furnished when we realize, the pieces set out on Josephine's polished floors were in the admirable new fashion France hailed as "Empire": we know what epoch they reconstructed, *which* empire had originated their classic curves. Napoleon's having in mind Augustus, imperial laurels, so-far-similar fortunes, led to Josephine's furniture and dresses being modeled as closely as possible on Livia's. Further, these two, each to the taste of a man of destiny, played their parts accordingly—each entered a drama at, as it happened, a point at which she could be at her best, do her best, contribute from what she was and had. Livia and Josephine were stylish; each knew how to give an air of heroic *chic,* of summery enterprise, to an enforced new order. Empire is an involvement: against glories the cautious are bound to balance possible cost. Ostentation, in young-imperial circles, could have made exactly the wrong impression. Livia and Josephine were elegant on an apparent shoestring.

There the resemblance stops. Josephine's losing of

Napoleon must, though dynastic necessity gave it cause, have been also due to mistakes such as love can make—one might say, such as only love *can* make. To love makes one less clever. Livia's mistakes, it would seem, were few (their annoying fewness may have accounted for her not being widely or warmly liked) and, such as they were, not in regard to Augustus. Are we to argue, she did not love him?—"the rising man" may be one thing, the man another. He and she remained an alliance—on his side, the closest his nature knew. Caught in the rapids of success, they were at least never swept apart. In return for the risk taken, she could hardly have made him a better wife. Augustus became a man with little to spare: that state, she probably understood, or (if after all she did love him) became resigned to. Livia, for her part, had much to steer: if she calculated (as her critics suggest), appeased, where necessary, too openly, obstructed friends who would gain the Emperor's ear, or seemed devious, automatic, or over-charming, can one blame her? Part of the situation in which she found herself was this: there was increasing tension, disaccord aggravated by circumstances (such as the childlessness of her second marriage) between her son Tiberius and his stepfather. Tiberius, first of her sons by Claudius Nero, was "difficult"—why he became so has filled books. Dislocated father-attachment, resentment against his mother for changing husbands were added to, as he entered manhood, by a sense of being thwarted and overlooked. For years, no appointment found for him seemed to him of enough importance, though the preferment shown him annoyed others. Augustus's lack of enthusiasm for Tiberius could have had sufficient domestic cause. But the objection had also a deep base—the failure of a son of his to be born, the failure of adopted heirs to survive, made it clearer to Augustus, with every year, that this psychological Caliban must succeed him. Between these two men of hers stood Livia, striving to make each hour and day agreeable. Were there times when she put her hands to her head, moments when she would have given anything, everything, to be elsewhere? There can be no woman, in anything like Livia's position, for whom Elsewhere is not at times the desired land.

Not for her, *villeggiatura* in the distant hills, whose blueness she saw from the tired Palatine. Augustus must never be out of call. The Prima Porta villa, though some way north, was so placed as to be absolutely accessible—a messenger had but to leap from his spent horse and sprint, if breathlessly, up the small hill. The Via Flaminia passes directly under the villa, through a cutting. This must, I thought, when I took stock of the place, have been like living over a main railway-line, or in America, for instance, the New Jersey Turnpike. Something was very wrong if two-way traffic along the Via Flaminia ceased to be ceaseless. There would be, of course, military interruptions: Augustus, looking up from his papers, would with knowledgeable ear check on the marching-rhythm of one of the legions. Did the Empress go to the villa door to breathe or look round the country, guards sprang to the salute. She did not walk in the country; to do so would have been highly peculiar—had the caprice seized her, it would have converted itself into an expedition, maidens with lyres, porters bowed under paraphernalia it was considered she might want. And what can a wood be but a disappointment, full of thorns, full of flies, full, after all, of nothing but many trees—what a bore, how hostile! What you saw in a wood, from the outside, vanished the minute you set foot in it. Somebody coming after her— "Madam, a word with you, if you please—" So she turns home, if indeed she ever went out. That was enough of it: between the real earth and real sky there is no Elsewhere. Once from her carriage she thought she saw . . . but she was in a hurry. One day, in the villa at Prima Porta, she thought of devising something-or-other for the oblong room. It was simply a matter of hiring an artist. She always knew where to go; she hired a good one, and he no doubt worked to specification. He may have been one of those educated slaves, in which case she had no more to do than put him to work. What happened next was quite unforeseen—she inspired the painter. It is thought that women inspire by their beauty; more often they do so by their longings. The execution was his, but the wood hers: he, though pleased with the wood when it was done, may have been puzzled by it—as he sauntered round, giving valedictory brush-flicks here to a petal, there to a feather, it may be that Livia screamed out: "And what are *you* doing here?—GO!"

That there was more to Livia than the wearied *soignée* woman I feel sure. She had to keep going; one does so from some secret resource. She had courage, and a grace one should not think less of because she practised it. The serene manner in which she lived down scandal (in spite of constant reminders from Tiberius) is to be admired—and I like her for some equivalent of humour, some perhaps lightly ironical way of seeing things, through which she kept individuals in play. She may have been the first person who made Augustus laugh, which would be an event he never forgot. She was a very Roman woman, quick in eye and faculties, living in the fingertips through their touch. What did she look like? She must have been the subject of many portrait-busts, of which some must be in the museums seen by me, but I have forgotten them. My sense of her physical being comes from a statue, said to be her, I saw in a villa—the figure sits slid forward, almost reclining, on a low, low-backed chair, in great ease, indolently at peace with its own beauty. It is young-mature. The *plissé* dress, having fallen vaguely around the breasts, flows on, moulding the narrow thighs, down the longer stretch between knee and sandal-tip. The repose suggests rest after something done, so well done or pleasurable in itself that it is to be thought over with a smile, in so far as the lady is thinking at all. The smile is in the attitude, or is a sort of effluence from the body: there is no head.

Livia seems very contemporary, seated here in the villa, by a window. Had she her head, were the hour dusk, one could take her for one more of the guests. Her modish fluid outline reminds me how favourably she would have looked on, how loved to sponsor, today, her city's great dress-designers—she is owed place in this latest empire of Rome's, fashion. Window-gazing along the Via Condotti, I see her in the subtle profusion behind the plate-glass, in the enchantedness lent to luxury, in the intricacy of tiny boxes and large necklaces, in the musically carven jades, crystals, corals, ivories, in the cobwebs of lace no less than the sharp-cut rays from jewellers' cushions, in the sheer *look* of scentedness. Ensnare Rome must: it has an aspect—this—which I find myself calling "the smile of Livia."

V

THE SET FREE

ON FEBRUARY 8th, 1849, there was proclaimed, again, a Roman Republic. A Constituent Assembly had been summoned; Mazzini spoke—"We must act," he said, "like men who have the enemy at the gates, and at the same time like men who work for eternity." Through Rome, dazed in the months foregoing by the speed of events (Pio Nono gone, in refuge in Naples with King Bomba), ran a wildfire of renewed belief—*had* there ever died out at least the power to regret, which in a sense is the power to believe, if only in the past? From today, there was to be not a looking back but a looking forward. Not that this was the first time the flame had been re-lit, and had burned; if only, it might appear, to be once more smothered. Promises have an honour in themselves, even if they are dishonoured later, when they speak to the better desires within people. One may play upon pride only, but the returns are short-lived. There *is* desire for virtue. In the Middle Ages, the corruption and failure of Rienzi had been a downfall, also, for those who stood by watching him hacked to death: the tragedy had been the obliteration of his original bright great concept, the Good Estate, with which had gone the declaration of a Republic—filling the streets of Rome on a May day, 1347, with the young of all ages, surging round the bare-headed, wonderful-looking young Rienzi in armour, and his two banners newly emblazoned with Justice, Liberty. It was to be a beginning with no end. One might say, always the same story: the backwash of scepticism, reaction, despondent or frivolous acquiescence, followed by the oblivion Rome finds or can feign to find so easy. But there had been that day.

Five hundred and two years later, the Mazzini occasion was more sober: rows of threadbare dark suits gathered in the Assembly, the faces upturned above them harsh with intentness. The day was not May but February; the speaker, with his disproportionate forehead, had no more beauty than he had egotism. If he fired hearers, it was by invocation—

speaking, as he did to the Assembly, under the impact of his return to Rome, that hour of which he wrote, later: "I entered the city, one evening, with a deep sense of awe, almost of worship. Rome was to me, as in spite of her present degradation she still is, the Temple of Humanity."

1849 was the first overt act in the struggle which terminated, victoriously, with 1870. There were watchers for whom the scene in Rome had political rather than patriotic colour: its connection, for them, with the year before, revolutionary 1848 with its simultaneous disturbances throughout Europe, was alarming. The expulsion (as it was seen) of the Pope justified an immediate battle-cry. All but all the 1848 movements to unseat power had outcomes which made them seem premature. "Say not the struggle naught availeth," urged the English poet—but how difficult not to, with England filling up, in the mid-century, with more and more of the Continent's disarmed revolutionaries, in exile and with, it seemed, few prospects other than more of it. To Mazzini, shortly to join their number, further part in the struggle was denied—when again, after ten years, a day came, he was not considered to be the man for it. Movements outgrow the visionary and need the strategist; Cavour, playing off power against power, steered the Risorgimento to its goal; there was to be no further reference to Eternity, other than as a claim for the glory of the dead. The more concrete half of Mazzini's February 1849 saying to the Assembly was, at least, soon to be given point to: April saw the enemy at the gates. It was a wonder, which certain disputes explain, that the delay had been even so long.

It was the French, finally, who took it upon themselves to "restore order"—an order in fact notably well kept: Rome had gone on its way quietly under its Republic, whose instatement had, but for one unpreventable incident, been bloodless. If, up to April, there had been citizens who were passive, critical, dubious if not dissentient, it took no more than the French to weld the new-made Republicans together. Battle was to be given: on April 27th in rode Garibaldi at the head of his Legionaries from South America. Never can Goth, Visigoth, or Ostragoth have looked stranger in, or to, the Eternal City than did these barbarians marshaled for its defence. For our friends the artists, onlookers, what models! Gibson the sculptor described "the spectacle offered by these wild-looking warriors as they rode in . . . the men, sunburnt, with long unkept hair, wearing conical-shaped hats with black, wavy plumes; their gaunt, dust-soiled faces framed with shaggy beards; their legs bare; crowding around their chief, who rode a white horse, perfectly statuesque in virile beauty."

Garibaldi struck at the French on April 30th.

The French were taken by surprise. An advance

force, still, it seems, tentative in intention, they had
made their way unhindered in from the coast and
taken up their position on the Janiculum, west of
Rome, above the Porta San Pancrazio, among beautiful villas with dreamlike settings. The Villa Valentini was their headquarters. This crown of the hill
(not to be confused with the spine along which runs
the glossy modern avenue with the lighthouse) had
been the nobility's pleasure-garden; the villas, less
than an hour's carriage-drive up from Rome, were
built less for sojourn than visitation—enlarged pavilions, rising storey on storey like stucco card-
houses, open to breezes, perfect for summer revelry.
In April, picture the glades emerald green, veiled by
delicious hazes in early morning, hollows sweet with
white violets among the mock-antiquities of the
Villa Doria Pamphili. If such charms spoke to the
French, the hill no less pleased their military realism: it was, as Rome's garrison also knew, for at-
tackers *the* strategic position—overtopping the
defending wall, having below it the city open to
view, and, if necessary, bombardment. The weak
flank had been always this, on the west. This time,
the French sense of advantage was to be fleeting:
Garibaldi had them out by the end of the day—dislodged from the Valentini, driven back, fighting
hard, from garden to garden, cut off from one another and shot down along the twisting avenues or
among the violets. By the evening of April 30th, the

birds scared from the groves were back; the French were in retreat to Civitavecchia. That night, Rome blazed with thanksgiving candles in windows; hand clasped hand, to the sound, through to dawn, of singing and cheering. Those most moved, like those still wary, were silent.

Danger had only begun. May had to be spent by Garibaldi campaigning in the Alban hills against Neapolitan forces moving up from the south: he inflicted two defeats on them—none too soon, for before the month had run out the French were back again; that was, reported moving on Rome, in strength this time, under command of Oudinet, with a long train of heavy artillery. Oudinet sent word, ahead, that he would not attack before June 4th: as he saw it (though Rome did not), that did not preclude him from capturing the vital Janiculum position in the small hours of June 3rd. Before daybreak that Sunday, the news reached the tricked city, though not, immediately, Garibaldi—who, sleeping it out, in preparation for the morrow, in a friend's house, was wakened by the bells already ringing furious warnings from every steeple, and drummers drumming citizens back to arms. Taken by surprise . . . Buckling on what he seized, alerting what men he could, he rushed up the Rome side of Janiculum hill, short-cutting from level to level up steep steps, sheer banks, stony breakneck footways. Tracing his course, one can all but hear the exasperated panting of his lion lungs. Not a halt for breath till the Porta San Pancrazio. From under its arch, straight ahead, you look—Garibaldi stared—ahead up the short road to the Villa Doria Pamphili gates. The gates, at the end, face you. The road, or countrified street, is a pleasant stretch between garden walls—at the worst glaring, for nothing shades it. Nothing did so that June. Nothing projects by an inch; nothing offered cover to the wave after wave storming their way up it under continuous fire from the French, whom the Doria Pamphili gates now masked. This was death alley.

Along the right of the road is the ruined ground-floor of one of the big villas, today roped together, apparently, by wisteria. Near the doorway forever hangs a laurel wreath, desiccated by sun; and there is a plaque with an inscription. *"Few against many, without hope of victory . . . the not degenerate sons of Rome and Italy."* The men who joined Garibaldi, when he landed from South America in Italy, had awaited only the call and a commander. Some had met before, others been separated till now by spied-upon frontiers or impassable mountains. Those setting eyes on Rome for the first time found themselves shoulder-to-shoulder with Romans born: the coming to being of this army in itself accomplished Unification. The volunteers' lives, now alike pledged, had been lived differently: poets, lawyers, doctors, noblemen, teachers, farmers were among the fighters. Fame awaited many, though not all. Looking from one to another of the faces of Garibaldi's "Hundred," whose statues line the Janiculum avenue, one thinks of the many others not here in marble, but names forever in the valleys or villages they came from. And in the Roman Republic's 1849 stand against assault, civilians also took eager part: on and onward from June 3rd students and artists streamed up from the city to man the wall. Women carried the eatables, wine, and water they had lugged uphill from bastion to bastion, staying to join in the laughter (of which at the beginning there was much), the mockery of the enemy, the brave holiday, till it was time to be down into Rome again, ransacking kitchens, taverns, and stores for more. For long there had not been such a Sunday. Along the ramparts, on the grassy embankments inside the fortifications, spirits were high. This section of wall, on the Janiculum, is not the Aurelian; the Papal wall with its large projections is still more massive but, here, less lofty.

That the French, with their fine revolutionary history, should be heading the forces of reaction was now shocking: Roman sense of enormity found voice in a manner as loud as it was ironical. Near the bastion from which roared a Roman battery, another, next the Porta Pancrazio, was occupied by

199

a lusty amateur band which did not cease to thump out *La Marseillaise,* singers bawling around it at full lung—

> *"Le jour de gloire* EST *arrivé!"* (pom-pom!)
> *"Contre nous de la tyrannie*
> *L'étendard sanglant est levé!"* (pom-pom-pom!)
> "L'ÉTENDARD SANGLANT EST LEVÉ!
> *Entendez-vous dans les campagnes*
> MUGIR *ces féroces soldats?"* (pom-pom!)
> *"Ils viennent jusque dans nos bras"* (pom-pom!)
> *"Egorger nos fils, nos campagnes.*
> AUX ARMES, *citoyens!"* (pom-pom!)
> "FORMEZ *vos bataillons!*
> MARCHONS!" (pom-pom!) *"Marchons!*
> *Qu'un sang* IMPUR" (pom-pom!)
> "ABREUVE *nos sillons!"* (pom-pom!)

Impossible to march: one could always stand! Did the sound reach the French, in between the firing? Taunting is a Roman art. Was this also, from some hearts, the sending up of a flare to the lost brother?

The epic, hopeless "battle of the villas" was fought, each inch, by the Garibaldians as though victory *were* possible. Forced, as June went on, down and down the Roman side of the hill, as bombardment shattered one frail stronghold after another, they left behind them war-ploughed gardens and pathetic wreckages of stucco. Roadside Villa Vaschi (on whose stump hang the laurels) once soared, pictures show, to fantastic height, and wore the air of belonging in Cytheria. That the Villa of the Four Winds (dei Quattro Venti) ever existed might be forgotten, did not a commemorative arch, in the Forum manner, proclaim its site. The human tempests to rage through and round the villa made its name more apt than its builders foresaw: sharing the park of the Villa Doria Pamphili (in which the French were), it stood nearer the gates, to which the Garibaldians had forced entry. Pivot of the early days of the fighting, the Four Winds, though vulnerable to fire from its neighbour, was at any price worth holding: it provided base and some kind of cover for the Italians' persistent short-range attacks. Inside the high saloons painted for pleasure, the air was white-misted by dust from the falling plaster, which stung eyes and turned faces to chalky masks. Across the windows the Garibaldians stacked up their dead, then fired across them—outdoors, for days together, the fallen, useless, could do no more than corrupt in midsummer sun. No Castor and Pollux, shining horsemen, saved this battle for Rome: the time was not yet—but the cavalier Nino Bixio, heading a fresh assault, galloped his horse with a shout up the outside staircase, charged through the *salone* and out again on to the balcony on the other side, head on into a hail of bullets.

In turn, the Villa Savorelli (now Aurelia) high above Porta Pancrazio, too good a target, had to be abandoned for the Spada, further down near the

Acqua Paolo fountain. Meanwhile the French, re-inforced, took up further positions round Rome and declared siege—during which, from the Janiculum, from outside the Porta San Paolo and from Mount Parioli they opened up simultaneous bombardments. Heavy shelling made a breach in the wall at last; while the enemy swarmed through that, in the dark and confusion, there were scalings and entries at other points. Rome therefore surrendered on June 30th. The Republic ended. "Order," which was to say the Papal Government, was restored promptly: the French remained to support it, throughout its final phase of watchful repression, vengeful ferocity (the dark 1850's pictured by William Story) till, in 1870, they were called elsewhere. Garibaldi, after negotiation, was allowed to withdraw his forces from Rome. On an early-July evening they lined up, laid down their arms, and, watched by the weeping people, saluted the city. He then marched his men off into the dusty sunset, though not forever.

For the time being, so much for 1849. The good in the struggle had been, moral resurrection. (The term is Sir George Trevelyan's.) There had been an accumulated dishonour to throw off. In some quarters, there were those sorry to see it go; and I know those for whom it has never gone. Rome, as I noted, provides a perpetual target for disapproval, in part ambiguous, in part not. The bringing of retrospective charges against it still goes on; it is possible to point to its days of glory's bad institutions, wrong tolerances, and/or the vices those bred or pandered to—cruelty, despotism, greed, indolence. Inhumanities accepted by ancient Rome do not show up well to our eyes; Christianized Rome, during many centuries, has hardly been better seen than its pagan forebear—people cease picking on the Emperors only to turn their attention to the Popes. Present-day Rome has guests who busily probe, then expose the results in regretful books. It occurs to me, looking at what I have written, that I may seem light in my attitude to Rome's failings, or wilfully blind to them. That is not how I am. Defects hurt one, hurt when one is made aware of them in oneself, and no less, I think probably more, when they force themselves into notice in what one loves. I have yet, however, to find the dismay they cause either eased by complaint or lessened by being aired by discussion. Much about Rome was a pity: leave it at that. I am sick of the governessy attitude of our age, which is coming to be more genuinely presumptuous, nosier, and more busybody than the Victorian. Deplore the past if you wish; you cannot do anything about it, other than try to see it does not recur. It can, and so far has—and each recurrence is worse; there is less excuse for it. Put the present to rights, by all means— but begin at home. Much about other peoples, nations who are our contemporaries, is a pity, but does it devolve upon us to tell them so, or say so in terms they may overhear? In cases of history, we may not be seeing things quite as they actually were, down the long perspective; nor is it only after time has elapsed that mistakes occur. We the democracies, for instance, are surprised by the stated totalitarian view of us—we are, we learn, given over to luxury, the enslavement of the worker, power-mania, whoring, boredom, imperialism, unseriousness, dyspepsia, blood-lust, insecurity, venality, money-making, sloth, intrigue, competitiveness, terror of wrath to come, servile art, sleeping-pills, hangers-on, steriliz-ing fantasies, degeneracy. Really, they make us sound like the ancient Romans.

Cruelty. Prominence has been given to those "without natural affection, implacable, unmerciful." We know cruelty to be of two kinds, that arising from lack of imagination, or stupidity, and that devised and inflicted by perverted imagination for its own reasons. The latter is clearly the more pernicious; the former, more general, apt to be more continu-ous, is not always the easier to endure, and may be exasperating to contemplate. Of that kind, in gen-eral, was Roman cruelty. One has yet to find a society which does not contain large, if not prepon-derating numbers of stupid people, whose power for harm is not as limited at it should be—*how* it is to be limited is a problem not yet solved. Slavery,

an institution taken over by the Romans from pre-
ceding civilizations (for which it had worked
well), could make for cruelty, did so, did not do so
invariably: the maltreatment of slaves was not only
uneconomic (in the sense that it deteriorated property) but contrary to a Roman law, which could be
invoked. Awful stories out of the past of England
show that the technically "free" servant, in particular
the young waif or orphan, ignorant, nobody's business, terrified of being thrown out, had less defence
against bad mistress or master than had, in the days
we consider, the "owned" slave. Technical ownership of one human being by another is a finished
evil; virtual ownership will go on until the wish or
predisposition to *be* owned is outrooted—how? The
slave was provided for. The slave did not need to
think; should he choose to do so, thereby burdening
himself with will and character, he had a future
ahead of him—the possibility of buying freedom, of
having it handed to him in recognition of his merits
and services, or of exercising the character he had
acquired, the influence he desired to put forth,
within still-existing nominal bonds. As we know,
the tutors, secretaries, household artists who im-
parted intelligence to a Roman family, knew more
of its business affairs than it did itself, or made
known to it a degree of aesthetic pleasure, generally
were or had been slaves. There are different ways of
acquiring gifted persons; the forthright Roman paid

a cash sum down—the creative or learned from subject countries were shipped in and offered for sale
in Rome. On any level, the slave developed abil-
ities. Slavery as a system was criticized by the contemporary thinking Roman, on two counts—that it
engendered indolence, to the point of atrophy, in
owners, who became unable to lift a finger for themselves, and that it made for the demoralization of
the "free" proletariat, who, out of demand as wage-
earning workers, became an increasing burden on
the State, having to be subsidized and placated. For
the indigenous artisan, there was little encouragement to acquire skills in which the imported slave
already excelled. For centuries, the worst of Rome
was the existence of thousands of people without
function, and the nature of the attempts made to re-
sign them to or distract them from their condition.
Nor were the useless of one class only. The Flavian
gift to Rome of the Colosseum signalized that no
place of popular entertainment could be too capacious, and no spectacle, for which ultra-ingenious
mechanism was herewith provided, too monstrous
in its appeal to sensation. Not everything staged in
the arena, under the vast tent-roof, involved bloodshed, or the shame, terror, or inexplicable courage
of unwilling participants, but it was considered a
poor day if there were nothing whatever of the sort.
One can think of no surer way of keeping people
down—and by "people" I mean the audiences. Prac-

tically everybody, fashionable or seedy, flocked to those entertainments: they saw no reason to stay away. "Triumphs," in which the glory of the general and his marching cohorts, impassive as ever after victory, was added to by paraded captives biting upon bitterness, wound their way clear of the Forum's turn-out of voracious onlookers, up the Capitoline to Jupiter. A world of orderly victors, with that outlook—above it, the blindfolded eyes and bland brow of Justice. Impartiality stood in the place of pity. Man must settle with man: "The law is open . . . let them implead one another." Hearing was accorded to anyone anywhere under the rule of Rome; distinctively greater were the rights of anyone who was a Roman citizen. Citizenship was a status which could be granted, held, irrespective and also without loss of the original nationality. Many who held it dwelled in outlying parts of the Empire; it ensured recognition, as does a passport, in any other part—entitling one to declare, "I am a Roman." It connoted freedom. Acquired by a father, the status could be inherited by his sons; those not fortunate enough to have inherited it could purchase it, though, clearly, those "free" for more than one generation considered themselves the better placed. It carried with it the right of appeal to Caesar.

See, in the Acts of the Apostles, the case of St. Paul, Jewish, a former Pharisee, "born free" in Tarsus in Cilicia, and the number of conscientious persons, whether of the civil or military authority, to whose troubles he added as he passed through their hands. Trouble had been already occasioned in Asia Minor when the saint arrived in Jerusalem for Pentecost. In Philippi, "a colony," the magistrates, pestered by complaints from the masters of the soothsaying girl, stupidly took action without enquiry; then, scared by the ominous earthquake which broke the prison into which they had cast St. Paul and his friends, sent word, " 'Let those men go.' " St. Paul would have none of that. " 'They have beaten us openly, uncondemned, being Romans, and have cast us into prison; and now do they thrust us out privily? Nay verily; but let them come themselves and fetch us out.' And the sergeants told these words unto the magistrates: and they feared, when they heard that they were Romans. And they came and besought them, and brought them out, and desired them to depart out of the city." In Achaia, where St. Paul was hustled by angry Jews from the synagogue to the judgement seat of Gallio, the deputy governor took his stand on the ruling Roman distinction. " 'If it were a matter of wrong or wicked lewdness, O ye Jews, reason would that I should bear with you; but if it be a question of words and names, and of your law, look ye to it, for I will be no judge of such matters.' And he drave them from the judgement seat." In Ephesus, the size and noise of the riot raised by the silversmiths, threatened with loss of trade should a slump occur in images of the city's patron goddess Diana, thanks to St. Paul's teaching, brought an official hurrying to the spot. Diana's reputation, he made haste to point out, was absolutely unshakable, above danger. If the silversmiths had a true case against the strangers, let it be brought— "The law is open." If his first concern was to appease the people, one cannot blame him: should this breach of the peace come to superior ears, *he* would take the rap. " 'We are,' " he agitatedly said, " 'in danger to be called in question for this day's uproar, there being no cause whereby we may give an account of this concourse.' ". . . Nothing so far, however, had approached the violence of the scenes in Jerusalem: here was unpent upon St. Paul the accumulated fury of his accusers, inflamed by rumors from Asia Minor. He had been warned— " 'They are informed of thee, that thou teachest all the Jews which are among the Gentiles to forsake Moses, saying that they ought not to circumcise their children, neither to walk after the customs. What is it therefore? The multitude must needs come together, for they will hear that thou art come.' " The multitude did come together; St. Paul was dragged from the temple. "And as they went about to kill him, tidings came unto the chief captain of the band, that all Jerusalem was in uproar. Who immediately took soldiers and centurions, and ran down unto them: and when they saw the chief captain and the soldiers, they left beating of Paul. Then the chief captain came near, and took him, and commanded him to be bound with two chains, and demanded who he was, and what he had done. And some cried one thing, some another, among the multitude: and when he could not know the certainty for the tumult, he commanded him to be carried into the castle. And when he came upon the stairs, so it was, that he was borne of the soldiers for the violence of the people."

For a Roman garrison, all in the day's work; they no doubt stood by for trouble on native feast-days. The commander hoped, for a minute, that he had killed two birds with one stone— " 'Art thou,' " he asked St. Paul, " 'that Egyptian which before these days madest an uproar, and leddest out in the wilderness four thousand men that were murderers?' " He was not; he was a Jew of Tarsus, "no mean city," and he requested leave to address the people. The commander, seeing a further chance to discover what this was all about, granted it—it was, however, in Hebrew that St. Paul spoke, from the top of the staircase, identifying himself, giving his credentials, together with an account of his education "at the foot of Gamaliel." He was, he reminded his audience —stilled, at the outset, by one of those hysterically intent silences which can fall on crowds—" 'taught according to the perfect manner of the law of the fathers, and was zealous toward God, as you all are

this day.' " So far, so good; the Romans stood by.
But the speaker next moved on to dangerous ground,
introducing the story of his conversion, then the still
more inflammable matter of his call to the Gentiles
—whereat the crowd snapped, howled, tore its
clothes off, and threw dust in the air. The Romans
withdrew St. Paul. What now? Here they were, with
this character on their hands, in custody—indeed,
given the temper of Jerusalem, protective custody;
not under arrest; one can be arrested only upon a
charge; the charge to be brought must be formu-
lated. The commander hoped to establish at least
something by putting the character to "examination"
implemented by scourging. St. Paul waited until he
had been bound for scourging, then asked the centurion, " 'Is it lawful for you to scourge a man that is
a Roman, and uncondemned?' " The centurion has-
tened to the commander— " 'Take heed what thou
doest, for this man is a Roman.' " The commander
hurried to the cell— " 'Tell me, art thou a Roman?' "
St. Paul said yes. The commander, staring mystified
at the scarecrow figure (who looks like much, when
lately beaten up by a mob?), was surprised into his
famous admission: " 'With a great sum obtained I
this freedom.' " It cost the earth to become a Roman;
he should know, for he had. St. Paul's rejoinder
sounds supercilious. Arrangements for the "examination" were swept away, as though they had never
been. Next day the saint, on his bettered footing,

spoke to a high-level deputation invited to the fortress: Ananias the chief priest, chief priests, scribes, Pharisees, and Sadducees. He took the offensive, calling Ananias a whitened wall; for that, someone struck him across the mouth before the Romans could intervene; unmoved, he went on to divide the party, invoking the Pharisees (his sect) against the Sadducees. " 'We find no evil in this man,' " the Pharisees ended by declaring. Violent become the dissension; the Romans had again to withdraw St. Paul. That night, he was told by God he must go to Rome. Next day, he was visited by a nephew who informed him of a plot against his life—he was to be lured from the Roman keeping by a challenge to dispute openly in the temple, seized on his way thither, assassinated by zealots who had sworn neither to eat nor drink till they had his blood. He insisted that the commander interview the nephew and hear the story. Claudius Lysias (for such, at this point, his name transpires to be) decided that he could cope no longer; the thing was beyond the domain of a plain soldier. He therefore despatched St. Paul, under heavy guard against attack on the road (two hundred men, mounted, with a horse for the saint), to the governor of the province, in Caesarea. One of the two centurions bore this letter:

Claudius Lysias unto the most excellent governor Felix sendeth greeting. This man was taken of the

Jews, and should have been killed of them: then I came with an army and rescued him, having understood that he was a Roman. And when I would have known the cause whereof they accused him, I brought him forth unto their council: whom I perceived to be accused of questions of their law, but to have nothing laid to his charge worthy of death or bond. And when it was told to me how that the Jews laid wait for the man, I sent him straightway to thee, and gave commandment to his accusers to say before thee what they had against him. Farewell.

(An outstanding mis-statement in this letter puzzles one as to the character of Lysias. It was *not* "having understood that he was a Roman" that he saved St. Paul from the violence of the crowd. Far from it: that his prisoner was "a Roman" had taken time to hammer into his head. Ignorance made his behaviour, one might consider, the more exemplary: his action showed the conditioned reflex of any responsible Roman on tribal territory—stop rioting; that is most quickly done if you detect and remove its cause. What, then, makes him untruthful in his account to Felix? I conclude, it dawned on him, in the interval between the rescue and the sending-off of the letter, that his act had enraged not merely a mob but influential Jews in the highest quarter, who might lodge a complaint against him in Caesarea. (He was right.) Lest his zeal be censored, it looked better to have intervened on behalf of a supposed "Roman" than on that of a nameless vagrant or native agitator.)

Felix committed himself in no way. Pending the arrival of the accusers, he turned St. Paul over into the keeping of Herod, the local king. When, five days later, Ananias and his Jerusalem party made their appearance in Caesarea, they were reinforced by the notable advocate Tertullus—who, upon the opening of the hearing, winningly addressed the governor. " 'Seeing that by thee we enjoy very great quietncss, and that very worthy deeds are done unto this nation by thy providence, we accept it always, most noble Felix, with all thankfulness. Notwithstanding, that I be not further tedious unto thee, I pray thee that thou wouldest hear me of thy clemency a few words. For we have found this man a pestilent fellow, and a mover of sedition among all the Jews throughout the world, and a ringleader of the sect of the Nazarenes.' " Now here *was* a charge. Felix (we may imagine) started rubbing his chin. Tertullus then got in the side-cut foreseen by Claudius Lysias. " 'Whom we took,' " he went on, meaning St. Paul, " 'and would have judged according to our law. But the chief captain Lysias came upon us, and with great violence took him away out of our hands.' " Tertullus's clients assented; all that had been said was certainly so. St. Paul, given the sign to answer, point-blank denied disturbing the peace: he had

disputed with no man, in the synagogue or elsewhere, in any manner likely to raise the people. He
accredited the trouble to mischief-makers from Asia
Minor—who should, he uncompromisingly said,
also today have been present before the governor.
" 'Or else,' " he went on, " 'let them here say
whether they found any evil doing in me, while I
stood before the council. Except,' " he turned to the
Sadducees, " 'it be for this one voice that I cried
standing among them, touching the resurrection of
the dead, that I am called in question by you this
day.' " Felix, at this point, announced he could go
no further without Lysias. He adjourned the pro-
ceedings, and they remained adjourned throughout
what was left of his term of office: he does not appear to have sent for Lysias. St. Paul, placed in the
easy keeping of a centurion, was meanwhile allowed
to receive friends and profit in any way from their
ministrations: among his visitors was Felix, who, accompanied by his Jewish wife, invited him to speak
of the faith in Christ, and on one occasion, we learn,
trembled. It is suggested that Felix kept in touch
with St. Paul out of hopes of receiving a bribe to set
him free. When, after two years, he was succeeded
in Caesarea by Porcius Festus, the outgoing governor left Paul bound, to please the Jews. Men make
concessions before departure, from the wish to be
favourably remembered.

Festus inherited the St. Paul problem from his

predecessor. No sooner had he shown his face in Jerusalem (to which he made the expected official progress three days after arrival in Caesarea) than the high priest and his company were upon him, clamouring. What they urged was, that St. Paul be returned to Jerusalem. Festus, though more than anxious for good relations, was obliged to see that this might not do. Instead, he desired the Ananias party to reopen the matter in Caesarea: he himself would shortly be back at the seat of government. Accordingly, the scene in the Caesarea judgement hall resumed itself; the "many and grievous" complaints were again poured out, Festus making still less sense of them than had Felix. St. Paul had had two years in which to reflect on the situation: he was on guard against the sedition charge, trailed past the Roman notice by insidious Tertullus at the earlier hearing. To his answer, " 'Neither against the law of the Jews, neither against the temple,' " he this time added, " 'nor yet against Caesar, have I offended any thing at all!' " Festus fancied he saw a loophole. " 'Wilt thou,' " he put it to St. Paul, " 'go up to Jerusalem and there be judged of these things, before me?'

"Then said Paul, 'I stand at Caesar's judgement seat, where I ought to be judged: to the Jews I have done no wrong, as thou very well knowest. If I be an offender, or have committed any thing worthy of death, I refuse not to die: but if there be none of these things whereof they accuse me, no man may deliver me unto them. I appeal unto Caesar.' "

Festus conferred with advisors: no way round this. Leaning back, let us imagine, not impossibly fidgetting for a minute more with the noble garments of office draping his shoulder, he resigned himself to the utterance of words which by being spoken became irrevocable. " 'Hast thou appealed unto Caesar? Unto Caesar shalt thou go.' " Enormous, impartial, patient, unstoppable machinery was to be set in motion. Was this, then, not an "out" for Festus? Anything but. Arrangements for transport for the defendant, under military escort, from here to Rome, with shipping conditions uncertain, were, though tedious and finicky, but a detail. The headache, for the unhappy governor, was the preparation of the document which must precede, go with, or swiftly follow St. Paul to the precincts of Imperial justice. How this hung over him night and day appears in his conversations with King Agrippa, who, coming to Caesarea just about now, with his queen Bernice, to pay the compliments due from regional royalty to the new Roman governor, stayed on: the two became the confidants of their hard-tried host. Out, after one or two evenings, came the worry. " 'There is a certain man left in bonds by Felix . . . the chief priests and the elders of the Jews informed me . . . I answered, it is not in the Roman manner to deliver any man to die, before that he which is accused have the accusers face to face . . . I sat on the judgement seat . . . they brought none accusation of such things as I had supposed, but had certain questions against him of their own superstitions, and of one Jesus, which was dead, whom Paul affirmed to be alive . . . I commanded him to be kept, till I might send him to Caesar . . .' " The king's reaction could not have been more welcome to the governor: Agrippa expressed a desire to hear St. Paul. The "command" hearing, though involving arrangements for full pomp, attendance of chief captains and notable Caesarea citizens, took place without delay. Festus seized the occasion to take the distinguished audience into confidence. " 'Ye see this man. . . . When I found that he committed nothing worthy of death, and that he himself hath appealed unto Caesar, I have determined to send him.' " (There was no option.) " 'Of whom' "— round again came the bother— " 'I have no certain thing to write to my lord' " (Nero). " 'Wherefore I have brought him before you all, and especially before thee, O King Agrippa, that, after examination had, I might have somewhat to write. For it seemeth to me unreasonable to send a prisoner, and not withal to signify the crime laid against him.' " *Unreasonable?*—it was out of the question. Such an omission could end the Festus career. "Somewhat to write . . ." From behind the bluff there issues a cry. The extent to which Festus's nerves were frayed shows in the violent crudity of his interruption. St. Paul was nearing the peroration of a discourse, never more reasoned, temperate, or lucid, addressed and in content levelled towards the attentive monarch who had invited it, when Festus shouted— " 'Paul, thou art beside thyself; much learning doth make thee mad!' " The saint, turning a tolerant eye upon the governor— " 'I am not mad, most noble Felix, but speak forth the words of truth and soberness' "— had the room with him. " 'The king,' " he explained " 'knoweth of these things.' " The king did; how strongly he had been acted on was to show in a minute. " 'Almost' " Agrippa declared to Paul, " 'thou persuadest me to be a Christian.' " All present were comprehended in the tremendous answer. When the king, the queen, and the governor withdrew, breaking up the assembly, Festus had the benefit of his guest's opinion. " 'This man might have been set at liberty, had he not appealed unto Caesar,' " Agrippa said.

The thing went forward. A ship having been found, St. Paul and other prisoners were placed aboard it, in charge of Julius, a centurion of the Imperial guard. Julius's treatment of the saint was courteous, deferential, throughout considerate. This fourth Roman to enter the story shows in a more pleasing light than the others; in fairness to the others it must be said that Julius was the only one for whom St. Paul did not create a predicament. The centurion had had his orders; he acted under them. He was to see that St. Paul reached Rome and be there delivered to the proper authority: he did so. The liberties he accorded his honoured prisoner were based on an understanding never abused. That they both so nearly never reached Rome at all was due to the excellent centurion's one stupidity—his support, after the party changed ships at Myra, of the idiotic captain of the next vessel, in face of a vigorous protest from St. Paul. Romans were unwilling, therefore not intelligent, sea-goers; their marine achievements and naval triumphs were few; they submitted, when enterprise urged or duty required, to being transported from shore to shore. St. Paul, on the other hand, knew everything to be known about sea-travel: one is struck by the fact that his many journeyings had hitherto been accomplished without a hitch. Among the trials he now endured must have been not having arrangements under his own control. In Julius's too great faith in the ship's captain we see one trait of the professional Roman: regard for professionalism in any form. The decision to make a dash from The Fair Havens, a natural harbour, for Phenice, said to be more commodious, there to winter, was crazy, given the time of year—the great gale season. Winds had been contrary already; further ominous weather-signs had been noted by the foreboding saint. But, on they went.

We know what befell the ship, seized upon by a diabolical wind called Euroclydon, battered, soon hopelessly out of course, with sun, stars, gone from the dreadful sky. Among the two hundred and seventy-six aboard reigned despair and chaos. At the height of the chaos St. Paul appeared, saying, " 'Sirs, ye should have harkened unto me. . . .' " Having been so far human, he went on the exhort and hearten—there was to be, he assured them, " 'no loss of any man's life among you, but of the ship.' " That had been told him: an angel of God had stood by him in the night saying: " ' "Fear not, Paul; thou must be brought before Caesar: and, lo, God hath given thee all them that sail with thee." Wherefore, sirs, be of good cheer; for I believe God. . . . Howbeit, we must be cast upon a certain island.' " From then on, command was his, Julius being his able second. It came to St. Paul's knowledge that captain and crew planned to abandon ship, leaving the passengers to perish: the centurion (whose opinion of mariners must have been now at zero) sent soldiers just in time to cut loose the boat in which the getaway was about to be made. Rammed (as a last hope) at the unknown shore, grounded, the ship was beginning to break up: soldiers came to Julius saying it would be better to kill the prisoners, lest in the confusion they should escape, swimming. The centurion, "willing to save Paul," put a stop to that. (Query: should he not have done so on principle?)

To the foretold island, which they found was Melita, all came safe, swimming or washed in on planks: *not* a life lost! The literal centurion, counting heads, saw a new dimension in his extraordinary charge. To prophecy fulfilled were next added miracles: the viper episode, the succession of healings which made that winter memorable for the barbarous islanders. Julius, not a barbarian, would have been more rather than less amazed: what went on beneath his Roman decorum? He is last heard of, at the end of the journey, securing privileged treatment for his chief prisoner. Lysias, Felix, Festus, though not clement, had attempted to act fairly: that was their *métier*. Like that great number of others serving under the Roman system, they had taken its stamp. Less good than the system, they were the better for it. Beyond it they saw little. They lived on earth during a crisis of other than earthly history; round them, the air quickened with what they wot not of. Lysias was given occasion to prevaricate, Felix to tremble, Festus to shout uncouthly. So far, however, no realized fear or anger distorted the Roman outlook: limited it was.

The party left Melita on a ship which had been wintering at the island. Called *Castor and Pollux,* she had as destination the coast of Italy. At Puteoli, where they landed, St. Paul and his friends were allowed to tarry with brethren seven days. What then remained of the journey was by road. Spring would have come to the country, speaking in one way to the strangers, another to those for whom this was, at last, home. Whatever beauties surrounded him, I cannot imagine St. Paul, at this stage, looking anything but burningly straight ahead—even when, towards the end of that endless last stretch, sunset melted over the Campagna, then without a ruin. Thickening in the distance, in the dust from chariots and dusk from gardens, began to materialize the city, trimmed with the topmost flashes of gilt spokes. As he neared it, friends who had heard the news and come out to meet him were waiting along the Appian Way. Seeing them, he thanked God and, as a commander needs to do, took courage. The well-made military road, ahead, afforded itself to the steady tread of himself and his little band. He advanced on Rome.

In tombs round the city lay those for whom a question had not arisen. Acceptance or rejection had not involved them. St. Paul was sent by God to the Gentiles "to open their eyes, and to turn them from darkness to light." Throughout his discourses, teaching, and writings is the stress on vision—as a faculty, in the optic sense. Loss of his sight, for three days, after the blaze of light on the road to Damascus, gave him to know in body what blindness was, to contemplate what in spirit it had amounted to. After that, could he forget the miracle which caused, instantly, scales to drop from his eyes? Nothing could be the same again. Christianity is a revolutionary insistence upon seeing, seeing anew—it was in that sense that it was a threat to Rome, to the maintenance of observances and conformities which, built into the system, indeed, its build-up, had to be seen in (only) the Roman way. How inevitably limited that way was, how much unseeingness went with it, we have noted. What aroused mistrust with regard to Christians was not their conduct, against which little could be brought, but their attitude, felt to be subversive. St. Paul's promise to go to Rome was of long standing; meanwhile, he had written and sent from Corinth the Epistle to the Romans— that was, to the Christians within and of the city: "called," he reminded them, "to be saints." Much of this Epistle wrestles with the question of sin: we come, at one of the points in the close argument, on these words, "He that is dead is freed from sin."

The crowded, sunny cemeteries of Rome have an air of freedom. Evidently belonging to the dead, they all the same give the impression of being overflows of livingness, which is in them stilled and transmuted by having entered these waiting pools. When we, living, speak of the "peacefulness" of such places, we mean the effect on our senses of returned innocence. They do bespeak mortality, but in commemorating the farewells paid to it and its burdens. How complicated, not less so for being shot through with pleasures, the sojourn on earth was, is; how much of earth's time we inevitably waste—but Eternity writes off the loss. In the large Campo Verano are laid many bound, in their day, to take life soberly: *of* Rome, as it is or has lately been, they lived embedded in large, observant families and extensive, important social connections, maintaining what was necessary for position, exacting what was due to them in respect, making or conserving money, housed, for the greater part, in regions of the city or its suburbs which, exploring them, I found more solid than gay. As compensation, there now, here, is something approaching gaiety in the surroundings; in the jump of the little flames in the ruby glass lamps, the gestures of high-spirited marble angels, the positive glitter of so much whiteness, the prettiness of small children rendered in effigy down to the last lace frill on a little girl's dress or curl on the crest of a little boy's head. There is well-awardedness, and there is non-finality—in the look of perpetual expectation in the eyes of young people, photographs glazed on to their grave-stones over the stories of laurels early won, not long worn on earth, sons at propitious starts of careers, daughters whose nuptials were all but celebrated. The Campo Verano monuments have among them vagaries according to taste, and sentiment—none to be mocked at. Up or down steps, round corners or through archways endlessly you may pass from section to section:

walls are lined with magnificent porch-type tombs, each a family's private entrance to the Hereafter. The display is grand; as afternoons yellow to evening the walks and alleys fill with admiring Roman strollers. Nearby is the basilica church of San Lorenzo, also the gate of the same name.

Near the San Paolo gate, inside the wall, are enclosures more visited by strangers. The part of the Protestant Cemetery one must enter first is not sunny, light being shuttered off by the high, close cypresses along the many paths, and evergreens diaphanous in the plots between them. Creepers, planted on the graves to betoken memory, interlace ironwork and entwine the monuments, which have lost whiteness as though saturated by dusk. This is Rome's permanent foreign colony. All looks neo-Gothic, not sad but naïve. Many of those buried here, one recalls, once dreaded the rigours of Roman sunshine: here is ensured for them the protective shade that in life they sought. They know better now. The tops of the trees are hummed through faintly and evenly, whenever I am there, by a mild wind which seems captive in this place: fancy could call it a sigh from shores never seen again. Pressing back the leaves to read the inscriptions, you learn how many nationalities are gathered here, how different were the stories, the countries come from, the forms of faith—the interpretation of "Protestant" is wide. Years have gone by, by the settled look of the place, since there last was a funeral; the aisle-like walks are trodden by pilgrims, no longer by mourners. Evergreens are rustled by patient searches for one or another grave, a long-ago relative's or revered compatriot's—signposts direct one only to the illustrious. Apart from Shelley, whose heart snatched from the pyre on the beach is buried at the top of the slope, under the wall, and Trelawny, who indefatigably arrived by his friend's side after half a century, those here may be taken to have the distinction of having died in Rome: they are one, in that case, of having had the happiness of being alive in it, whether for a long or short time. Whatever happened, I count them fortunate.

Not so Keats, fortunate in regard to Rome only in the lovely position of his grave—out in the other, open part of the cemetery, to which one passes through the dividing doorway, from shadows into the sun. The room he died in, held to the last in arms of Severn, looked out sideways on to the Spanish Steps: the tread of people going up and down, voices, laughter rendered demoniacal by the hearer's fever, must have mounted, all days, most of the nights, to the low window; though, given the sum of the agony, what more mattered? That small room, today lined with relics and bookcases, is not easy to enter. This is only one of the sufferings Rome has known, I think, standing in the middle of the floor, but it is enough; it was too much. He died, he wished it to be recorded—and he drew no breath, before he did die, to recall the wish—"in bitterness of heart." If that be sin, surely for him the pain of it was atonement? Keats's innocence is the sweet air over the grave, in spring a source of daisies and wild anemones, which flower out from it over this whole calm close to the foot of the Pyramid of Cestius. The pyramid has cats for ever moving around it, on it, or yawning, or basking on their genius for nothingness. From within one parapet rise two headstones: JOHN KEATS *is* to be read, but not on the poet's. His friend has joined him. Dear Severn's epitaph lodges for the painter one first claim: he had been the friend of an immortal—*who* that was, Severn's stone blazons out. At the top of the other, nothing but a lyre; near the foot, the final words Keats desired: "Here lies one whose Name was writ on Water." The pair of Englishmen have few neighbours in this fresh, desultory grassy stretch; it is natural to wander to see who the few are. Among them, two let us imagine beautiful Irish sisters, Miss Moores, from and of Moorehill, County Waterford—Helen, dying in Rome at eighteen, was three months later followed by Isabella, aged twenty-nine. The elder nursed the younger, then caught it, too? 1805, Moorehill lost its daughters; sixteen years later, Earth lost Keats. No, lost he could not be! Death does nothing to poetry. The loss, for us, is that of the "more": otherwise, does it matter whether a poet, being what he is, is alive or dead? It could be said that the Miss Moores, being nothing but themselves, were the greater loss.

It matters, to those of his time, who knew him and expected to know him longer, whether a young man is alive or dead. That you must feel, walking about the British Military Cemetery—further along inside the Aurelian Wall, overlooked by Monte Testaccio. Of the soldiers under the ranks of crosses, how many thought to enter these walls, or thought of them at all? Rome was a name on a map. They came to it not of their own wish; it was a matter of the fortunes of war, which mean, the course taken by a campaign. They had other ideas. There was a time, not so long ago, when they could as easily have imagined themselves dead as in old Rome. Nor did they need to; most of them were not called on to set living eyes on it. Most of these four hundred and twenty-two fell in the 1944 fighting approach. The graves, uniform under keeping, cannot all have been visited by families—a long journey from England, simply to put down flowers and stare, without knowing what to say, at one cross among so many the same. Nevertheless, "Rome" has come to mean something, wherever the homes are that the boys came from—it means the boy, whichever and whoever he was. And fathers and mothers and wives or girls, invited to add in their own words to the historic inscriptions in the city, did so: the messages they hesitated and consulted over, then sent out, have been written on the crosses: "Goodbye Jim," "Proud of you, Son," "We'll see you again, when the skies are blue again." Climb up Monte Testaccio, and from its windy top look around you—travelling with your eyes from the military cemetery (where some other tiny walker may have succeeded you) to the part of the river where, below you, the busy docks were when Rome was its own considerable river port—which means long ago. The Tiber's curves are to be followed, from up here, into either distance: this may be a day when they are shining. If this be a day when light paints Rome, from here you see what it can do. Look down the slope on another side: workers, in a sort of village, are measuring, slicing, and planing Rome's ever-needed marble into sheets for facings, propping them as they finish them, one by one, up against the decrepit shacks. This green high steep cone you are on, Monte Testaccio, is less old than Rome; it began as a dump for broken earthenware, and of nothing else, under its topsoil, is it composed. Well, is it called a mount, for it mounted up; its height is 115 feet—it *feels* like earth, wonderfully firm to stand on. *Amphorae,* emptied of what they had held when they were unloaded, were customarily knocked to pieces, as useless, which they had become, then cast out on to the heap, year after year. A sad trade, surely, to be a potter making short-lived *amphorae*. However, they made a hill.

* * *

Going out and coming back played an even greater part in my time in Rome when that neared its end than they had at the beginning. What had been a two-way means of discovery now helped to stave off the idea of departure—the day it could not. Outings are a distraction. I may have got it into my head that I could ease myself into being away from Rome by being so for hours together: if so, that did not work. But the spring was being extremely beautiful—drawing out for instance a smell of violets (never in reality found by me) from the silenced green streets and tree-grown courtyards of Ostia Antica, and returning a tang of the sea to the lost port, left behind by the coastline, deserted by the river. Ostia Antica, why, I cannot think, looks anything but forlorn; I have never seen more prosperous ruins—many look like buildings going up; roofless it's true, jagged down one corner, but only so far. "*That* will be handsome!" one is often on the point of exclaiming. The place has the best of both worlds; it is also poetic, spread out there on the flatness, untroubled, outlined by marsh light. If people knew what was good for them, they would be setting up house here again (not allowed, I expect), taking advantage of the fine theatre and the shopping-centres, dispersing themselves in the orderly airiness of the forum. This once thriving mercantile city as well as port enjoyed, by all signs, circumspect luxury—it deserves a day or very long afternoon; there is much to see, nothing that one *must* see, which is what I like. Loafing about Ostia Antica is justified by its being an example of Roman town-planning: the nearby capital might have looked like this, in a larger way, had there been less fuss, less pressure of population, and no hills.

Anxiety to see what Augustan Rome as a whole did look like was one of the reasons for my excursion to the "1942" Exhibition, where a model vouched for as perfectly to scale and correct in detail was said to be on view. It was shortly to *be* on view: subtle distinction—I badly bruised a shoulder battering-ramming it against a locked, high, horrible bronze replica of an ancient Roman door; I afterwards learned that had been the wrong one, but as the right one together with all others was locked also, what matter? I was really frightened by where I found myself: alone, so far as my eye could see, in the heart of the vast shell of this exhibition which had never taken place. What happened to be a tense, grey, gloomy, and eerie March afternoon accorded with the spectral avenues, seeded along their cracks with desiccated grasses, and the Fascist-classical architecture looming round me. Heaved high on arcades, down which draughts wandered, the buildings were cased in marble white by nature but shaved so thin as to let through a bluish death-hue. Within, the arcades were sheeted with dusty plate-glass, through which it was just possible to see into showrooms in which nothing had been shown, and where nothing showed, now, but musty patches making maps on the walls. What had been intended to go on in the floors above, one could not conceive. The horror of the whole mock-city, with its rows upon rows of square-cut, staring, unmeaning windows, was its emptiness—never had it known or contained anything else. I thought of the year 1942, and of all that had happened, other than this. From behind some blocks there reared up the silhouette of a stadium, appearing only a little less large than the Colosseum, though unfinished. Good Lord, deliver us—He did. The lower part of the place, I found, as I came down the steps from the bronze doors, fondling my shoulder, was not quite unfrequented: at one corner a brave glass café was open, with a couple hunched over a little table with their coat-collars up, sipping at something; a custodian-watchman, in the course of one more of his disheartening rounds, paused to give me a stare. Then I saw a small dog, a sort of terrier, lame, evidently unowned. One of those sudden intentions lost dogs have sent it off down the perspective of the central avenue, dot-and-carry-one. (The model of Augustan Rome was, ultimately, given to public view on Rome's Birthday, April 21st, in the course of an august and quite cheerful *festa* which took place in a relevant corner of the Exhibition. The model was well worth going back again to see, even among crowds. It has near it, in its lit-up underground quarters, a section-by-section reproduction of the procession which spirals round the Column of Trajan—that is also rewarding; in real life one cannot see it from near enough.)

The dog was heading for what was literally the high point of the exhibition: an immense columbarium—structure consisting almost entirely of arched apertures. On each of its six floors, pierced by daylight, statues could be seen standing about; and the approaches were guarded at the four corners of its terrace by nude colossi, with Neanderthal foreheads and bulging biceps, each with a cubist horse. This is a landmark for miles—today, the irresponsible little Metropolitana railway train had put me off immediately underneath it, on the exterior side, so that I could nowise enter the exhibition without passing near it, which I was loth to do. Later, while I was gazing at it from the central square, a safe distance, I saw a long file of German seminarists, in their scarlet *soutanes,* sweep up the terrace steps and into the arches—the effect was, a trickle of blood reversed, returning to the wound. The next hallucinatory moment in the square was when a perfectly normal bus drove in, turned, and came to a stop. This was a terminus. So I got in and was rattled back into Rome that way, passing not far from the beautiful eucalyptus woods in which are the Tre Fontane. There it was, it is said, that St. Paul was beheaded: his head, flying from the block, rebounded three times, and as it did so from each spot welled a spring, never to cease to flow. Over each, in this still exceedingly quiet place, has been built a church. Try, on leaving the exhibition (if you go to it), to make your way straight to the Tre Fontane, to have the bad taste washed from your mouth. I wish *I* had done so, that first day; I did on another.

It is impossible, in spring, to walk too often on the Appian Way, under the cumulus piling into the blue. Spaced out along the wayside, the domestic-looking tombs and crumbling angles of former towers might seem, if often enough you pass them, to be keeping a look out for you. Company is something, for this is like walking on a causeway across a lake of emptiness extending on each side—the Campagna is *not* empty; why should it feel so? The further out you go, the fewer the cypresses and the flat-topped pines. For stretches together the road is treeless. Each tree serves to encourage the walker onward, as would a mile-stone—first sighted ahead, then gained, then left behind: were it not for that, one might doubt whether anything so little as one's step was taking any effect on the great distance. Of the skeletal, enduring old Roman villas you from time to time leave the road to explore, that of the Quintilii —two noble brothers murdered by a covetous enemy—is the most nearly complete and the most romantic. Ahead, a mirage of colour dissolved into air, or air into colour, is apt to tempt you out further than you know, till suddenly, less tired than dizzy, you have to drop on to grass verge; where you remain, plucking vaguely at the trefoil, not even thinking. If you wake from the daze to find it is late—"too late," that is—you sprint across to the Via Appia Nuova, along which glide speedy electric train-trams, stopping at concrete platforms. If in no hurry, ease yourself back on to your feet (which, if you have sense, on a day like this will be clad not in heavy "stout" shoes but the supple Roman kind: in those you have the easy sensation of walking barefoot, but for not fearing to stub your toes) and retrace your way to near Caecilia Metella, where, by now, pretty suburban ladies dressed for an evening in town are likely to be waiting. Then, home into Rome on the bus in the dusk.

Transport, such an opportunity to talk, reminds me how bare what I have written may seem of interchanges. Though not a travel book, this of mine, I suppose, can hardly hope for other classification, therefore is bound to be found to be lacking in I don't know how many ways; I *am* sure of one. Almost all other writers made significant contacts; they no doubt sought them. They gained insight from successions of conversations which they enliven their pages by recording. Even chance helped them; nobody they bumped into failed to say something not only memorable but symbolic or symptomatic, or sometimes both. The most trite bar never failed to have in it a fearless thinker; never did they flump

on to a bench but they had as neighbour a character
from whose lips poured ageless wisdom with a
regional tinge. I cannot fairly complain, for the
fault is mine: wherever possible I avoid talking.
Reprieve from talking is my idea of a holiday. At
risk of seeming unsociable, which I am, I admit I
love to be left in a beatific trance, when I am in one.
Friendly Romans recognize that wish. Country-peo-
ple, in the surroundings of Rome, are a dignified
blend of friendly and taciturn. I sometimes wonder
whether they suffer from exhilarated visitors—cou-
ples, for instance, of English ladies who think nothing
of legging it through miles of olives to converse with
anything in the nature of a *contadino,* however
busy, when they would not dream of interrupting a
Lincolnshire labourer at work. I did, as a matter of
fact, have a number of short but happy and warm
talks, punctuated by nodding and smiling, but I see
no point in writing them down—they were not, so
far as I remember, particularly illustrative of anything. Commonplaces are good to exchange, for
they soon give out. If I want information, I always
ask. On the whole I let Rome reel past like a silent
film, following what went on (as one did in those
days) with the greater, closer, more spellbound and
fascinated attention for the absence of explanatory
wordy sound-track. Little can people tell one about
themselves that one does not know, if one has
watched them. Sometimes, by listening-in, I caught

fragments out of exciting stories. I must be childish; what I principally want is to have stories told me, or questions answered. As it came nearer my time to go, I more and more studied the dear great family I was about to be detached from. Romans (I mean, those now about Rome) never sneeze, and wonderfully seldom laugh. When *I* sneezed, it felt like some dreadful incontinence. The membrane inside their noses must be different. Laugh, I realize they do do, but never nervously; it might be better to say that they never titter. A laugh in Rome may be a performance, involving, if it take place in a restaurant, a preliminary putting-down of knife and fork, or a taunt, or a form of incitement—or, naturally, it breaks out hugely after a joke, to the point of shaking everything round it. Otherwise, smiles do the work. In this city, they are a wide vocabulary.

I must not give the impression that I remained, for going on three months, locked in an interesting hush. My conversation, like ancient Rome's street traffic, was unpent at nightfall, when I went to dinner or other parties or out with friends. Handsome happy evenings became a second, other, Roman existence, an alternative story. I think one needs to be French to define, or evoke, those particular flavours of social pleasure, which differ according to where one is. Stendhal, painfully conscientious in his descriptions of masterpieces (if anybody could put one off the Sistine Chapel, he would), excels at giving the atmosphere of those Roman *soirées* which were, surely, the genuine solace of his stay. That, of course, was Rome of the 1820's. The diamond-sharp wittiness of cardinals, voluminous in the *salons* of expert hostesses, we see, set off by the velvety loveliness of young women—who, alas, it was found, would settle for nothing less than a grand passion. Rome our author considered less civilized than Paris, though for the better—for, "Civilization," he had decided, "blanches the soul."

While I stand and regard it, the indifference to myself shown by a work of art in itself is art. In Rome, I was more drawn to statues than to paintings. But, whether it was a statue or a painting, I came to recognize first a disturbance and then a lessening of the confusion within me as I beheld. Partly there was a liberation from the thicket of the self, partly some equivalent of St. Paul's sensation of scales falling from the eyes. In Rome, it was extraordinary how I woke up in the mornings to realize how much was near me, how near the edges of vision I had been sleeping. When it came to going round some of the churches and galleries to say goodbye, I found the goodbyes charged with the greatest sadness to be those to things I had loved, perhaps, more for reasons within me than for their absolute, own sakes. Perhaps "love" only settles on what is in mortal, not immortal? What I cared for

now, I might not care for so much if I came back
again—*if* I came back again? There, in the Villa
Borghese, I faced it that I might in a sense be looking my last on the snarl of David, twisted by the
instant before the letting go of the sling, or that
other Bernini, Daphne writhing within the clutch
at once of Apollo and her metamorphosis—while
you watch, bark rushes up her thighs and her twig-
fingers separate into leaves. But there need be no
end to the shimmer of the rooms, the ever-reflecting
floors, the marble halls in which one has the right to
dream that one dwells. The halls, the galleries—
whatever they were called, Vatican, Borghese, Con-
servatori, however far apart they might be in Rome
—ran together into the unbroken chain which had
led me, and had led others and would lead others,
on and on, in and out of the many Romes. So what
matter? All the same, I looked out of a Borghese
window at the flowers in the garden and began to
cry.

After Easter, there were two more Sundays, the
second my last. Before that, I had the honour of
being taken by a friend to the Beatification, in St.
Peter's, of the Christian Chinese martyrs massacred
during the Boxer rising. There were more people
than, seeing St. Peter's empty, one could have pictured even it capable of holding. Not only length
and width but great parts of the inconceivable
height were thronged, tiers upon tiers of galleries

having been constructed. Half the lights in the world were already blazing, hanging in torrents from the roof, clustered against the carmine brocades clothing the columns, when on the ungated river of congregation we surged in, scaled to our places, waited. Then, to a burst from the organ, so far more (it seemed) than the other half blazed out that, by contrast, we might have been waiting till then in dusk. The Pope's procession was moving up the aisle. Before Pius XII was carried a scarlet spiked tree of gladioli. This was his first other than brief appearance after the long bout of the illness he had fought: no so tumultuous and rejoicing a wave of love of thousands for one ever could ever have been imagined breaking, gathering up again, again breaking. Nothing could contain it. Drowning the loudening organ, the clapping and crying aloud went on and on, as Pius XII was borne slowly forward to the high altar, turning to bless us from side to side.

The last Sunday was very blue all day, very hot all night. The yellow of evening brightened on the upper parapets of the Pincio, making the dusk in the Piazza del Popolo below by contrast bluer and, though watery-clear, mysterious. Above, many coloured balloons afire with sun could be seen trailing against the sky, and a band was playing— loudly enough for those who preferred to circulate down in the *piazza* to be able to do so, also, to music. As shadow travelled up the face of the Pincio, I also

241

climbed the ramps and staircases to the festive terrace, to continue moving restlessly about. By now I was anxious to be gone, so as to have going away over. Crossing the gravel to an empty table, I sat down, soon to find myself drinking something I had never drunk, a glassful of some sort of coloured syrup. The waiter had misunderstood my order. Dust from the trodden gravel was filling the summery, tired air: as evening deepened, ilexes ran together ahead of it into the ink of midnight. Lovers wandered away from parties, deeper into the glades to await darkness, in which, when it came, their presences would be felt in the zones between lamps wakening in branches. I walked to the bridge spanning the deep gulch, one side the Aurelian Wall, between the Pincio and Borghese gardens, and looked over. Under me passed cars returning to Rome, people with elbows out of the open windows in what was already an August languor.

Two days later I left, taking the afternoon train to Paris. As before, I had too much baggage to go by air. Such a day, when it does come, has nothing particular about it. Only from the train as it moved out did I look at Rome. Backs of houses I had not ever seen before wavered into mists, stinging my eyes. My darling, my darling, my darling. Here we have no abiding city.

BOOKS READ

The History of the Roman World, B.C. 30–A.D. 138, by Edward T. Salmon (London: Methuen & Co.); *The Reign of Tiberius,* by F. B. Marsh (London: H. Milford); *Claudius, the Emperor and His Achievement,* by Arnaldo Momigliano (Oxford: The Clarendon Press); *Social Life in Rome in the Age of Cicero,* by W. Ward Fowler (London: Macmillan & Co.); *The Romans,* by R. H. Barrow (London: Penguin Books); *Roman Society from Nero to Marcus Aurelius,* by Samuel Dill (London: Macmillan & Co., re-published by Meridian Books, New York); *Daily Life in Ancient Rome,* by Jérôme Carpocino (London: G. Routledge); *Monuments of Ancient Rome,* by Dorothy M. Robathan (Rome: Bretschneider); *The Life of Benvenuto Cellini,* autobiography (London: The Everyman Library); *The Taste of Angels,* by Francis Taylor (Boston: Little, Brown and Co.); *Garibaldi's Defense of the Roman Republic,* by G. M. Trevelyan (London: Longmans Green & Co.); *Roba di Roma,* by William W. Story (Boston: Houghton Mifflin Co.); *Walks in Rome,* by Augustus J. C. Hare (London: G. Allen & Co.); *The Acts of the Apostles.* I record my gratitude to the British School and the American Academy, in Rome, for allowing me access, in their libraries, to maps, prints and engravings, and topographical monographs. My authority as to the wall, gates and roads of Rome is the late Thomas Ashby.

Also available in Vintage

Elizabeth Bowen

THE DEATH OF THE HEART

With an introduction by Patricia Craig

'A writer of genius'
Sean O'Faolain

It is London in the late 1930s, and into a coterie of rather grand early-middle-aged people the sixteen-year-old orphan Portia is plunged beyond her depth. Disconcertingly vulnerable, Portia is manifestly trying to understand what is going on around her and looking for something that is not there. Evident victim, she is also an inadvertent victimiser – her impossible lovingness and austere trust being too much for her admirer Eddie, who is himself defensive and uncomfortable in this society which has managed to bring them together. In the midst of the rising tension is set perhaps Elizabeth Bowen's most brilliant piece of social comedy, when, at a seaside villa full of rollicking young people, Portia experiences at least temporary relief from the misery Eddie seems determined to bring her.

'The moment when the general public first realised that here was a writer of outstanding gifts was on publication of *The Death of the Heart*, a poignant study of the destruction of adolescent innocence'
Daily Telegraph

V

VINTAGE

BY ELIZABETH BOWEN
ALSO AVAILABLE IN VINTAGE

Bowen's Court & Seven Winters	009928779X	£6.99
The Death of the Heart	0099276453	£6.99
Eva Trout	0099287749	£6.99
Friends & Relations	0099287757	£6.99
The Heat of the Day	0099276461	£6.99
The House in Paris	0099276488	£6.99
The Hotel	0099284758	£6.99
The Last September	009927647X	£6.99
The Little Girls	0099287781	£6.99
To the North	0099287765	£6.99
A World of Love	0099287773	£6.99

FREE POST AND PACKING
Overseas customers allow £2.00 per paperback

BY PHONE: 01624 677237

BY POST: Random House Books
C/o Bookpost, PO Box 29, Douglas
Isle of Man, IM99 1BQ

BY FAX: 01624 670923

BY EMAIL: bookshop@enterprise.net

Cheques (payable to Bookpost) and credit cards accepted

Prices and availability subject to change without notice.
Allow 28 days for delivery.
When placing your order, please mention if you do not wish to receive
any additional information.

www.randomhouse.co.uk/vintage

Basilica Sotterranea
p. 167